About Island Press

Island Press is the only nonprofit organization in the United States whose principal purpose is the publication of books on environmental issues and natural resource management. We provide solutions-oriented information to professionals, public officials, business and community leaders, and concerned citizens who are shaping responses to environmental problems.

In 1994, Island Press celebrates its tenth anniversary as the leading provider of timely and practical books that take a multidisciplinary approach to critical environmental concerns. Our growing list of titles reflects our commitment to bringing the best of an expanding body of literature to the environmental community throughout North America and the world.

Support for Island Press is provided by The Geraldine R. Dodge Foundation, The Energy Foundation, The Ford Foundation, The George Gund Foundation, William and Flora Hewlett Foundation, The James Irvine Foundation, The John D. and Catherine T. MacArthur Foundation, The Andrew W. Mellon Foundation, The Joyce Mertz-Gilmore Foundation, The New-Land Foundation, The Pew Charitable Trusts, The Rockefeller Brothers Fund, The Tides Foundation, Turner Foundation, Inc., The Rockefeller Philanthropic Collaborative, Inc., and individual donors.

AN INTRODUCTION TO
Coastal Zone
Management

AN INTRODUCTION TO
Coastal Zone
Management

TIMOTHY BEATLEY
DAVID J. BROWER
ANNA K. SCHWAB

ISLAND PRESS

Washington, D.C. • *Covelo, California*

Library of Congress Cataloging-in-Publication Data

Beatley, Timothy, 1957–
    An introduction to coastal zone management / Timothy Beatley,
David J. Brower, Anna K. Schwab.
      p. cm.
    Includes bibliographical references and index.
    ISBN 1-55963-280-1 (alk. paper). — ISBN 155963-281-X (pbk. :
alk. paper)
    1. Coastal zone management—United States.   I. Brower, David J.
II. Schwab, Anna K.   III. Title.
HT392.B43 1994
333.91′7′0973—dc20   94-13333
                                             CIP

Contents

Chapter 3 Coastal Pressures and Critical Management Issues 34

Chapter 4 The Coastal Management Framework 55

Chapter 5 Federal Coastal Policy 66

Chapter 8 Local Coastal Management   148

Chapter 9 Conclusions: Future Directions in U.S. Coastal Management   185

Acknowledgments

Several chapters of this book draw heavily on previous work of the authors. Specifically, Chapters 4 and 5 contain information presented in an earlier report on coastal risk allocation policy, prepared for the Office of Technology Assessment, U.S. Congress. The authors wish to thank OTA for funding this work, and especially Bill Westermeyer for his assistance and encouragement. Chapter 7 on regional coastal management uses material from a guidebook on Special Area Management Planning prepared for, and with funding from, the North Carolina Division of Coastal Management. Also, Chapter 8, which addresses local coastal management, is drawn heavily from an earlier guidebook on hurricane hazard mitigation prepared for the North Carolina Division of Emergency Management under a grant from the Federal Emergency Management Agency. The sections on sustainable development draw on work done under a grant from the North Carolina Sea Grant Program.

We wish to acknowledge with gratitude the help given to us in the preparation of this book. Dan Ashe and David W. Owens provided valuable insight and helpful comments during the long process of this book's creation. Duke University students Amy Romano and Jean-Pierre Plé provided background information relied upon in this book through their research on an earlier coastal zone management project. Many hours of valuable research were also put in by Jessica Cogan, a planning student at the University of North Carolina at Chapel Hill.

We wish to acknowledge the phenomenal word-processing skills of Carolyn Jones, as well as the secretarial services of Barbara Rodgers. We also greatly appreciate the solid administrative support provided throughout the project by Carroll Cyphert of the Center for Urban and Regional Studies, the University of North Carolina at Chapel Hill.

1

Introduction

The Importance of the Coastal Zone

The coastal regions of planet earth are amazing areas. The interface between land and sea, the coast is a unique geologic, ecological, and biological domain of vital importance to an astounding array of terrestrial and aquatic life forms—including humankind.

The importance and value of the coastal zone cannot be underestimated. It is one of the most productive areas accessible to people. Fish and other seafoods fulfill a significant portion of the dietary needs for millions of people around the world, while the industries of fisheries and aquaculture are commercial mainstays for thousands of coastal communities.

The coast also provides an important safety feature for residents living near the ocean. Many types of coasts provide a barrier from natural hazards emanating from the turbulent seas. Beaches, dunes, cliffs, and barrier islands all act as buffers against the high winds and waves associated with coastal storms.

The recreational aspect of the coastal zone is another factor for which we value the region. Stretches of beach and rocky cliffs along the Pacific and Atlantic Oceans and along the Gulf coast provide numerous recreational opportunities for thousands of Americans. Boating, fishing, swimming, walking, beach-combing, and sun-bathing are among the numerous leisure activities in which our society revels.

Many of us go to the coast for the sheer beauty of it. There is something restorative and regenerative about the waves crashing and wind whistling. The aesthetic and scenic elements of the coastal zone make it invaluable as a source of inspiration and peace.

The coastal zone also provides a unique habitat for thousands of plant and animal species. The coastal ecosystem is made up of myriad interconnected subsystems whose functions cannot be duplicated elsewhere. For instance, estuaries, with their unique mix of fresh- and saltwaters, provide a nursery area for numerous species of fish. Likewise, coastal wetlands are home to a variety of birds, plants, and other biota, and also serve the important role of filtering impurities in the water coursing through them. These and other segments of the coastal ecosystem are precisely balanced, fragile areas susceptible to a variety of threats, including those posed by human interference in the natural system.

Despite its fragility, the coastal zone is amazingly resilient. The ecosystem as a whole is a dynamic and regenerative force; if "left alone," natural mechanisms operate to maintain an equilibrium between all living things and the natural environment. There are limits, however, to the extent the coastal ecosystem can withstand external assaults to its integrity. Pressures emanating from the activities of people are particularly threatening.

The Pressures on the Coastal Zone

Natural Processes

There are many pressures exerted on the coastal zone every day. Some of these are part of the natural operation of coastal processes. Every day, winds and waves move material and affect the landscape. More dramatic action occurs with coastal storms, including hurricanes and northeasters, which can bring high winds and wave surge forceful enough to change the topography of the areas they hit, literally overnight. For instance, barrier islands are very unstable areas. Over time, in reaction to storms and the accumulative daily buffeting of winds and waves, the islands actually move; they are constantly migrating, usually landward. Inlets are another example of a coastal feature that is migratory in nature. Inlets can shift laterally, be closed entirely, and new inlets can be created during a particularly forceful storm.

Human Interference with Natural Processes

Such alterations in the landscape are part of the natural processes in motion in the coastal region. Coastal areas are dynamic, yet adaptable.

Changes in the natural environment are to be expected, and the region can recuperate when allowed to continue its evolutionary process. It is when additional external pressures are exerted on the coastal zone that the area cannot recuperate fully. Human interference with natural processes can alter natural dynamics. For instance, hard structures built up along the beach to prevent erosion (e.g., groins, jetties) can actually exacerbate the erosion problem by trapping sand in one area and preventing its natural lateral drift to areas downstream.

The Pressures Exerted by Humans

Just the fact that people live in the coastal area is a form of pressure itself. The coastal regions of the United States are some of our most attractive places to live, both in terms of economics and aesthetics. The resources of the coastal zone provide numerous job opportunities, and many people come to the coast for recreation. Population density is another measure of the stresses placed on coastal areas; when more people are using a limited resource, the carrying capacity of the region can sometimes be exceeded.

Both the numbers and the density of population can increase dramatically during the vacation season. During peak summer months the population of many coastal communities can double, triple, or increase even more. Increased leisure time, as well as a rise in disposable incomes and a penchant for travel, mean more and more Americans are spending more time at the shore.

Of course, people at the shore, both permanent residents and visitors, need to be housed, fed, and entertained. The pressures exerted by the presence of human beings at the coast emanates from these needs. Houses, hotels, condominiums, restaurants, gas stations, shopping malls, golf courses, piers, amusement parks—in short, development—is spreading along all reaches of America's coastline. All these various development projects require infrastructure—roads, bridges, parking lots, sewers, etc., each of which can exert pressures on the environment or lead to various negative impacts. For instance, the increased area surfaced by impervious materials due to development projects and the infrastructure supporting them can cause problems with runoff into surrounding coastal waters.

People also need potable water, and many coastal communities are largely dependent on groundwater for their supply. However, there is a limit to the quantity of groundwater that can be withdrawn at a certain location within a certain time without adverse impacts. The water needed to serve projected population growth cannot exceed the gap between current withdrawals and this limit. The cumulative impact of groundwater usage can lead to changes to the water table, resulting in saltwater intrusion. Groundwater can also become polluted through the introduction of organic and inorganic contaminants associated with human settlement.

Human pressure exerted on the coastal region also involves the disposal of waste. We have been using the oceans and the coastal zone as dumping grounds for years, hoping the assimilative capacity of the ecosystem will take care of the problem. Medical waste washed up on the shores of the East coast, for instance, has been known to close beaches for weeks. Barges filled with garbage have been unloading their cargo at sea for years, and not too far from the shoreline. While the recuperative qualities of the coastal region are high, over time the natural environment will not be able to withstand the pressures without serious alteration or degradation occurring. In other words, we are using the oceans and coasts as "sinks" for our wastes, and the sinks are filling to overflow levels at a rapid rate.

The Effects of Human Pressure

The effects of human-induced pressures on the coastal zone can be far-reaching and long-lasting. As noted above, human activity can interfere with the natural processes of the coast and prevent the ecosystem from maintaining the equilibrium so necessary to its continued vitality. Both the marine and terrestrial environments are tightly integrated systems in which all the parts are interrelated and dependent on one another. Destruction or degradation of one component can lead to impairment of other parts or the dysfunction of the ecosystem as a whole.

The cumulative impacts of human-induced pressures can be extremely significant in coastal regions. Until recently, cumulative impacts of development on the coastal ecosystem have not been regarded as a serious problem because human and development pressures have not for the most part overtaxed the assimilative capacities of natural systems. As the coastal population continues to grow, however, long-term cumulative impacts will become more evident. The adverse impact of a single project can sometimes be minimized to a certain extent. Considered together with other development projects, however, the single project becomes part of a much larger ecological problem. As more and more projects are permitted in the coastal region, and more are concentrated in popular and economically profitable locations, the cumulative impacts will undoubtedly grow.

Areas which possess sensitive coastal resources (e.g., wetlands, waterbodies, fish and wildlife habitats) are particularly vulnerable to cumulative impacts. Areas of the coast experiencing rapid population growth are also especially prone to cumulative impacts. Population is an important gauge because changes in size and composition of the population directly affect the amount and character of development in an area. Changes in population and development patterns impose new impacts and demands upon natural and built systems in the area. In addition, population change increases the significance of natural processes such as barrier island migration, sea level rise, or coastal storms.

The Coastal Zone as a "Hazardous" Area

The coastal zone can be a "hazardous" area. Hurricanes and other coastal storms have been known to destroy entire communities in a matter of hours. People are displaced, homes and businesses are destroyed, infrastructure can be uprooted, and human lives can be lost. But why do these disasters occur? Because people have put themselves in the way of a natural force that cannot be diverted or stopped. The coastal zone is hazardous because humans have made it so. Coastal storms have no power to create thousands or even millions of dollars in damage to property if no property is within the storm's reach; nor can a storm kill people if no people are in its path.

Of course, there are hazard mitigation practices which can lessen the impact of a storm on a coastal community. For instance, buildings can be designed and constructed to withstand all but the most forceful of winds and wave surge. Well-planned and executed evacuation measures can reduce the risk to humans by getting them out of the way before a storm hits land. But the fact remains that coastal areas are hazardous only when there is something at risk in the area, something put there by people.

Public Policy Exacerbates the Pressures

Many of our current public policies can exacerbate the pressures placed on the coastal zone. Without the intention to inflict harm, our regulatory and political structure nevertheless tends to encourage the exact type of behavior that endangers the fragile natural resources of the coastal area. The most obvious of these policies are those which encourage development in coastal communities. Such growth, which can actually increase the dangers to the environment, places more people and property at risk from coastal hazards.

For instance, infrastructure, a necessity for growth and development, is usually provided by various levels of government. Paved roads and highways, while ensuring safe transportation routes for local residents, also allow more people access to more coastal areas. Similarly, bridges can open formerly isolated areas (such as barrier islands) to numbers of people that may exceed the carrying capacity of that particular locale. Sewer systems and municipal wastewater treatment plants allow the density of coastal populations to increase dramatically. And the provision of public water supplies can deplete aquifer reservoirs at a faster rate than they can be replenished.

The availability of various types of hazard insurance is another form of encouragement for development in coastal areas. The availability of federal flood insurance in particular is frequently cited as a primary example of how hazardous coastal development is subsidized and how the wrong kind of incentives are created. Owners of property damaged by coastal storms and flooding are often allowed to rebuild in the same or equally hazardous locations. The damage-rebuild-damage cycle accounts for many damage claims, and there are no incentives for avoiding development in hazard-prone areas.

Coastal development subsidies are also provided in the form of tax expenditures, deductions, or other subsidies contained in federal and state tax codes. For instance, casualty loss deductions reimburse owners for damage to property that is not covered by insurance. Deductions are also allowed for interest and property taxes on second homes, typical of coastal development.

Alleviating the Pressures on the Coastal Zone: Sustainable Development

As discussed in the previous paragraphs, people's activities are placing burdens on the natural resources of the coastal zone beyond their collective capacity to absorb the impact without adverse reaction. Human society is now using resources and producing wastes at rates that are not sustainable. It is our nation's penchant for growth and our consumption habits that threaten the vitality, even the very existence, of a healthy, aesthetic, and productive coastal zone.

Although the presence of human beings has been the major causal factor in most of the environmental problems now being experienced in the coastal zone, *not* living there is not a realistic solution. We are not suggesting that all built structures be razed, all roads removed, and all people leave the coast. Instead, we as a nation must change our attitude as well as our behavior. What is required is a new way of thinking: humankind as a part of the system, not its master.

This new attitude could result in many innovative and complex solutions to the world's environmental problems; but one manifestation with large potential for actually changing human behavior and breaking out of the destructive growth cycle lies in the concept of "sustainable development." Presently, sustainability is a foreign concept to our growth-acclimated culture. We do not now view the earth and its resources as finite; but even "renewable" resources have the potential for becoming finite if used and managed with impropriety.

Sustainable development has become the catchword in the environmentally conscious nineties. There are many different definitions in current usage, no one of them accurately or fully embodying the two components—"sustainable" and "development," and the relationship between these oft-times dichotomous concepts. However, one generally accepted definition has emerged from the report *Our Common Future*, published by the World Commission on Environment and

Development (commonly referred to as the Brundtland Report): sustainable development is "development that meets the needs of the present without compromising the ability of future generations to meet their own needs." The Brundtland Report elaborates on its definition by stating that sustainable development is "not a fixed state of harmony, but rather a process of change in which the exploitation of resources, the direction of investments, the orientation of technological development and institutional change are made consistent with future as well as present needs."

Sustainable development does not mean *no* growth. It *does* mean not wasting resources; but most proponents of sustainable development realize that without some growth, communities would not be in a position to provide for their citizens a decent standard of living and engage in the newly required effort to improve the environment. Sustainable development does, however, demand a change in the content of growth, to make it less material- and energy-intensive.

While not every approach to sustainable development will necessarily encompass the same set of assumptions, some basic principles do emerge to guide our endeavor to reach development that is truly sustainable. All proponents of sustainable development emphasize that a greater knowledge and appreciation of, as well as respect for, the natural world is essential. To this end, education and consciousness-raising about our environment must be first and foremost. Furthermore, the active and full participation of all the citizens in the community is crucial. This includes an awareness of the destructiveness of current over-consumptive lifestyles. Participation in grassroots organizations can really make a difference in our lifestyles and habits. We must then go further and become involved in the political structure that shapes much of the policy regarding growth and development at the state, national, and international levels.

We must engage in efficient resource use, reversing the degradation of renewable resources and implementing strategies for the sustainable use of land, water, biological and genetic resources, and energy. Reducing waste generation, recycling wastes into productive activities, and finding safe ways of disposing wastes that remain are essential elements in creating a healthy and habitable world. Polluters should pay for the costs of remediation, but it is even more important to prevent pollution and waste of resources in the first place.

And finally, and perhaps most importantly, all human activity should be judged from its long-term environmental impact, not just from its short-term gain. The philosophical principle guiding sustainable development lies in its future orientation, without ignoring the needs of living people. An appropriate formula for determining whether an action lends itself to sustainable development may well be: "Will children be able to enjoy equivalent or better opportunities than their parents did?" (Beller et al., 1990).

The Rationale for Government Intervention

Each individual in our overly consumptive society must participate in the change of attitude necessary to achieve development that is truly sustainable. But in addition to the changes we must make in our daily habits and patterns of behavior, society as a collective body of individuals must change its attitude and actions as a whole. While we can speculate on a number of different methods of achieving this universal behavior modification, one method for which the institutional mechanisms are already in place is through governmental directive.

However, to achieve such an approach, we must overcome the strong aversion in our country to what is often viewed as overly intrusive government action, especially in the area of land use. Private property rights are deemed almost inviolate in the United States. However, much of the abuse we have inflicted on the natural environment has as its source the way we use and manage our land and the attendant natural resources. This is especially true in the coastal zone, where development is taking place in inappropriate areas at an ever accelerating pace.

What land use regulation does take place in the United States falls mostly within the domain of local governments. This traditional view of land use regulation being a local prerogative is in many cases a suitable one, since the function of regulator is necessarily site-specific. However, due to the nature of the coast and the coastal ecosystem, local governments may not have the capacity in terms of financial resources, technical ability, or political willpower to fulfill the role of official protector and conservator of the coastal zone. Natural resources do not necessarily conform to humanity's artificial political boundary systems, and ecosystem limits often transcend local jurisdictions. Many coastal environmental problems are regional in scope, and local governments may not have the authority to deal with such wide-ranging issues. Furthermore, local governments may have too parochial an outlook to be effective at implementing the theory of sustainable development community-wide.

Due to a realization that local powers are in large part insufficient to effectively manage the coastal region, state and federal governments have to some degree stepped in to fill the gap. This book describes several of the measures being undertaken to control land use patterns, use of natural resources, and human activities which impact the coastal zone. However, while well-intentioned, these federal and state programs are also found to be lacking. The traditional processes of government control and regulation have limited effectiveness, especially considering the long-term health and vitality of the coastal ecosystem.

What is needed now is a new and different set of values on which to base our government actions. Coastal zone management for the last two or three decades has focused on the catchword "balancing"—a balancing of economic development and preservation of the environment. This is all well and good, but we must go beyond balancing and operate under the theory of sustainability if we are to ensure that humankind's presence in the coastal region will not produce its demise.

This new approach to government intervention based on the principles of sustainable development calls for an integrated program of coastal zone management. The system must be operative at all levels of government and involve all the participants in the coastal region. Many of the tools are already in place; the regulatory authority and financial resources are in existence, should we choose to direct them to the appropriate needs. What is missing is the wisdom, the will, and the political foresight to create a management system which will protect, enhance, and preserve our coastal zone for ourselves and for future generations.

2

Understanding the Coastal Environment

The Special Nature of Coastal Areas

The human species seems drawn to coastlines. Recent population trends suggest that coastal areas are increasingly attractive places to live and work. Coastal areas are now more than ever called upon to provide recreational services, whether in the form of sunbathing on the beach, fishing, or bird-watching. Americans are spending more and more of their spare time frolicking in the coastal sun.

The reasons for our fascination with coastlines are probably many. Clearly, coastal areas represent immense natural beauty and provide unique aesthetic experiences. The sharp contrasts of sky, water, and land are exhilarating to many.

For others the coastline represents a boundary between the familiar terrestrial world and the immense and mysterious sea. As Barnes (1989) notes, "beyond it lies an essentially alien world on or in which we can survive for extremely short periods without the aid of technology." The fascination value coastlines have to many is further enhanced by the dynamic and rapidly changing nature of the coastal environment. One day it may be calm, the next stormy.

But coastal areas are ecologically complex and extremely dynamic environments that can be altered or destroyed by overuse by the human species. This chapter provides a very basic introduction to these physical and ecological features and dynamics and should give the reader a sense of both the importance and sensitivity of the coastal natural environment. The chapter begins with a general discussion of ways of classifying coastlines and some discussion of the geomorphology of the coast. The chapter then describes in some detail several

of the more important habitat types found in coastal areas, including
beaches and barrier islands, estuaries, and coastal wetlands. This is not
meant to be a comprehensive analysis of coastal habitats but rather a
selected overview of several of the more critical of these coastal environments. The chapter then goes on to discuss some of the most important physical forces and processes that influence and shape the
coast, including wind, waves, and sediment transport; hurricanes and
coastal storms; sea level rise; and the coastal hydrologic cycle.

Defining the Coastal Zone

An initial question is how we define the coastal zone and the area we
are concerned with managing in this book. We might approach a definition in several ways, either from a political-planning boundary or
from a physical point of view. Any physical or natural definition would
clearly include the very edge of the shoreline, for example, barrier
beaches along the Atlantic coast. But how far inland or landward do we
consider this zone to extend? The coastal zone is a transition zone, or
an ecotone, lying between oceanic environments (or lakes) and terrestrial systems. Most definitions rely to some degree on the extent of
tidal influence. As Hansom (1988) notes: "The coastal zone includes
the land-sea-air interface zone around continents and islands and is defined as extending from the inland limit of tidal or sea-spray influence
to the outer extent of the continental shelf."

Despite the need to establish some physical boundaries for the
coastal ecotone, it is important to remember that critical physical and
ecological interconnections extend beyond these areas, and that
coastal zones can be impacted significantly by human and other activities that happen at great distances away from the coastal zone. The
condition of coastal waters, for example, is clearly influenced by erosion and non-point-source water pollution that may happen many hundreds of miles upriver. The watershed for the Chesapeake Bay, for example, includes portions of six states, extending well beyond any usual
definition of the coastal zone. Yet soil erosion and nonpoint pollution
occurring along upland river areas have a major influence on the water
quality of the bay. Acid deposition, as a further example, threatens the
waters of the Chesapeake Bay as well, and is again largely the result of

activities happening outside of the coastal zone (e.g., coal-fired power plants).

Management or planning boundaries represent another way of de-limiting the coastal zone and may or may not correspond very closely with our physical boundaries of the coastal zone. State coastal zone management programs, for instance, have adopted different types of boundaries for a variety of practical and political reasons.

Types of Coastline

Coastlines around the world exhibit a diversity of physical types and characteristics, the result of major differences in geology and natural processes. Even within the United States, major differences exist. The Atlantic coast, for instance, is characterized by a system of barrier beaches and a relatively wide continental shelf. The Pacific coast, on the other hand, is characterized by a narrow continental shelf, limited barrier beaches, a mountainous coastal region, and tectonically active geological system (see Figure 2.1). The broad, flat coastal plain, as found along much of the eastern United States, in turn has allowed the formation of extensive coastal marshes, while few such marshes exist along the Pacific coast. Some coastal areas are heavily influenced by river systems, such as the Mississippi delta, and the extensive flows of sediments injected into the coastal system.

There are a number of different ways of classifying coastlines. One common way is based on the theory of plate tectonics, which provides much of the explanation for why coastlines have evolved in such dra-matically different ways. Based on plate tectonics, three types of coast-lines are frequently identified: (1) collision coasts, (2) trailing edge coasts, and (3) marginal sea coasts (see Inman and Nordstrom, 1971). Collision coasts are formed as a result of two plates colliding, generally resulting in straighter coastlines, narrower continental shelves, and tectonically unstable mountains. The Pacific coast of the United States generally falls into this category (Davies, 1973). On the other hand, trailing edge coasts, which are the product of two plates di-verging, generally result in a much wider continental shelf, larger river deltas, and more tectonically stable inland areas. The Atlantic coast of the United States falls into this category. Marginal sea coasts exhibit greater diversity of characteristics and have many of the features of a trailing edge coast. "They are frequently modified by fluvial plains and deltas, their hinterland may vary considerably in relief and their adjoining shelves vary much in width" (Davies, 1973, p. 12).

Coasts have also been classified according to the types of wave forces they are subject to. For example, some coastlines can be classified as storm wave environments because they experience short, high waves from all directions. Cliff forms are more common here, while depositional landforms are uncommon. Swell wave coastlines, on the other hand, are characterized by waves which are long and low and tend to

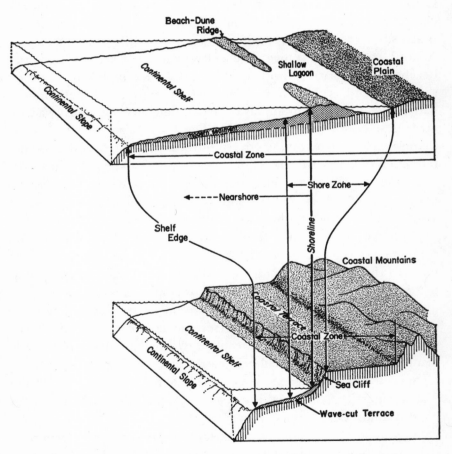

Figure 2.1   Wide-shelf plains coast (upper), characteristic of the U.S. East coast (trailing edge), and narrow-shelf mountainous coast (lower), characteristic of the U.S. West coast (collision edge). (From Clark, 1977.)

come from a consistent direction. As a result, beaches, barrier islands, and other depositional landforms tend to be more common. Finally, protected sea environments do not experience significant wave action because they are protected by ice cover (in high latitudes) or enclosed by land (Hansom, 1988).

These types of coastline classification systems are, of course, quite broad. Any particular stretch or segment of coastline will itself exhibit different features and geomorphology. As an example there is considerable variation found in the coastline of South Carolina. Brown has divided the South Carolina coast into four primary types (see Figure 2.2): mainland coast (arcuate), delta, sand dune ridge barriers (beach ridge barriers), and thin retreating (transgressive) barriers (as described in Neal, 1984). The mainland coast stretches from the North Carolina border to Winyah Bay and is characterized by a fairly stable, higher elevation coastline (the location of an ancient barrier island complex). The Santee River delta is another distinctive coastal type (Cape Romain, the largest river delta on the East coast). Two types of barrier island landforms are identified in Figure 2.2. The sand dune ridge

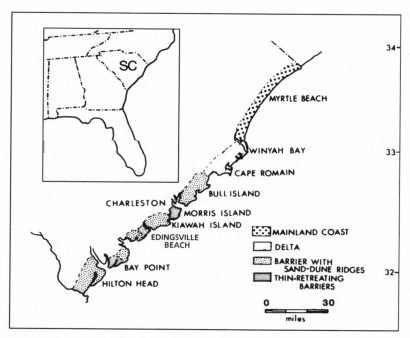

Figure 2.2 Classification of the South Carolina coast. Modified from a figure by P. J. Brown in *Terrigenous Clastic Depositional Environments*. (From Neal, 1984.)

landform includes the drumstick-shaped barriers, such as Hilton Head and Kiawah, which contain well-developed vegetated ridges. Thin retreating barriers, on the other hand, are thinner, rapidly migrating islands, without an extensive dune or beach ridge (such as Morris Island or Edingsville Beach; see Neal, 1984).

Types of Coastal Habitats

There are a number of distinctly different habitat or ecosystem types within the coastal zone as we have defined it, each suggesting unique management and planning requirements. A full cataloging or discussion of these ecosystems types is, however, beyond the scope of this introductory text. For a fuller and more comprehensive presentation the reader is referred to more detailed coastal ecology texts (e.g., Clark, 1977). The introductory discussion here is oriented toward several of the more important of these habitat/ecosystem types, including beaches and barrier islands, estuaries, and coastal marshes.

Beaches and Barrier Islands

Beaches and barrier islands are major landforms in the coastal United States and are the focus of much of the development and population pressure coastal areas are experiencing. Sandy beaches on the Gulf and Atlantic coasts are generally associated with barrier islands, but such a system of barriers does not occur on the Pacific coast.

The Gulf and Atlantic coasts of the United States are heavily characterized by a system of barrier islands, generally running from Maine to Texas. This system is comprised of about 300 different islands, and a combined oceanfront distance of 2,700 miles (see Figure 2.3). The system extends over 18 coastal states and comprises some 1.6 million acres (Dolan and Lins, 1987; Wells and Peterson, undated).

Barrier islands are formed of loosely consolidated materials, primarily sand, and are subject to forces of wind, waves, sediment transport, as well as the effects of hurricanes and sea level rise. These forces and the potential impacts on barrier islands are discussed in more detail below. Barrier islands vary considerably in size and width, but most can be characterized as low-lying and highly vulnerable to coastal flooding and storms.

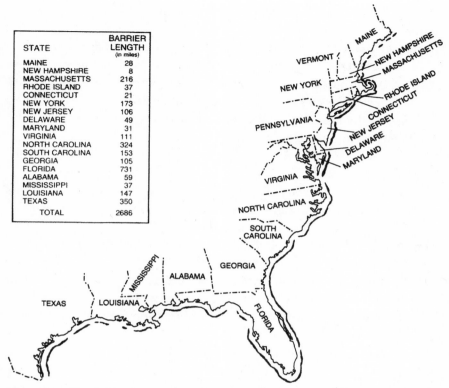

STATE	BARRIER LENGTH (in miles)
MAINE	28
NEW HAMPSHIRE	8
MASSACHUSETTS	216
RHODE ISLAND	37
CONNECTICUT	21
NEW YORK	173
NEW JERSEY	106
DELAWARE	49
MARYLAND	31
VIRGINIA	111
NORTH CAROLINA	324
SOUTH CAROLINA	153
GEORGIA	105
FLORIDA	731
ALABAMA	59
MISSISSIPPI	37
LOUISIANA	147
TEXAS	350
TOTAL	2686

Figure 2.3 Hundreds of coastal barriers (shaded line) protect the Atlantic and Gulf coasts. (From Wells and Peterson, undated.)

The explanation for the formation of the barrier island system has long been the subject of speculation. Most coastal geologists believe that formation and gradual landward movement have been closely tied to sea level rise. When the last period of major sea level rise began to occur approximately 18,000 years ago, wind-formed dunes were breached. As sea level rise continued, it is hypothesized that the islands gradually moved landward. While some barrier islands are experiencing accretion in the short term, the barrier island system as a whole is continuing to retreat, again largely in response to gradual sea level rise (Kaufman and Pilkey, 1979; Pilkey et al., 1980).

Barrier islands are themselves comprised of different and distinct ecosystems, depending again on their size and width. Larger barriers frequently contain primary and secondary dunes, interior wetlands and maritime forests, and salt marshes on the landward side (see Figure 2.4).

Barrier islands and barrier island systems, then, serve many important social and natural functions. They serve as the first line of defense against hurricanes and coastal storms, they provide necessary enclosures for estuaries and marshes, they are home to a variety of plant and animal life (including a number of endangered species), and they provide considerable recreational and aesthetic benefits.

Estuaries

Estuaries represent some of the most ecologically productive elements of the coastal environment, rivaling tropical rainforests in their primary productivity. Estuaries are those coastal aquatic systems formed through the mixing of freshwater from riverine systems and saltwater from the ocean. Prichard (1967) presents one of the more commonly cited definitions of an estuary: a "semi-enclosed coastal body of water which has a free connection with the sea and within which sea water is measurably diluted with freshwater derived from land drainage." The defining feature of an estuary, then, is its fluctuating salinity, and estuaries vary depending upon the relative dominance of freshwater or saltwater. This is in turn heavily influenced by the tidal range. Some estuaries, known as salt-wedge estuaries, are dominated by freshwater and have small tidal ranges and, thus, small marine inputs (Hansom, 1988); the Mississippi River is a major example of this type of estuary. Partially mixed estuaries have a larger tidal effect and smaller river flow, resulting in more pronounced mixing of saltwater and freshwater (with the freshwater usually on top and the saltier waters on the lower layers); the James River is an example of this form of estuary. Fully mixed estuaries have even stronger tidal flows and weaker river inputs.

Estuaries are also frequently classified by their geological origin and geomorphology. Most estuaries have formed as the tidal mouths of rivers. Consequently, they are often referred to as "drowned river valley" estuaries, and were formed as recently as 6,000 years ago in response to sea level rise (see below). The Chesapeake Bay estuary was formed from, and largely comprises, the ancient Susquehanna river valley (Lippson and Lippson, 1984). "Bar-built" estuaries represent a different type of formation. They lack the deep river indentation, are usually much shallower, and are separated from the ocean by barrier

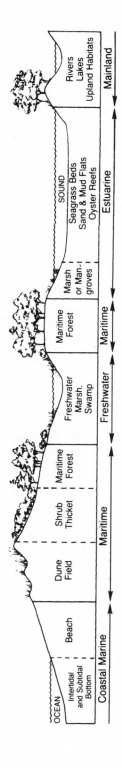

Figure 2.4 A cross-section of a well-developed barrier island and nearby mainland. (From Wells and Peterson, undated.)

islands and sand spits, with intermittent inlets (Knox, 1986). The Texas estuarine system is perhaps the best U.S. example of this type (see Figure 2.5). Some estuaries have been formed through tectonic processes (e.g., land subsidence and faulting, as illustrated in the case of the formation of the San Francisco Bay).

Estuaries exhibit plant life specially adapted to these saline conditions, including extensive salt marshes, mangroves, and eel grass beds. (Coastal marshes are described in more detail later.) Estuaries exhibit a tremendous level of primary productivity, and in turn serve as important nursery grounds for a variety of fish and shellfish.

Estuarine systems exhibit a complex food chain (e.g., see the diagram of food web and energy flows in Clark, 1977). Estuarine plants serve as direct food for certain animals (fish and shellfish), but more importantly provide small particles of decay (detritus), which are consumed by microscopic life (zooplankton), which in turn are consumed by fish and then by other animals higher on the tropic scale, including humans. This food web is often characterized in terms of producers (plants), consumers (plant-eating animals like zooplankton, oysters), foragers (those who prey on consumers), and predators (those who prey on foragers). (See Clark, 1977, for a more detailed explanation of the estuarine food chain.)

The ecology of the estuary depends heavily on the salinity gradient. Different species of plant and animal life are able to tolerate different levels of salinity. Interestingly, while the primary productivity (amount of organic matter produced) is greater in more saline or brackish portions of the estuary, species diversity tends to be lower (Thorne-Miller and Catena, 1991; Chabreck, 1988).

Coastal Marshes

Coastal marshes really represent an ecological subunit of estuaries. They represent a class of wetlands found, to some extent, along all U.S. coastlines. These are extremely productive habitats, formed primarily from river sediment and home to saline-adapted plant life. There are an estimated 9,440 square miles of coastal marshes in the continental United States, with most located along the Gulf and Atlantic coasts (Alexander et al., 1986; Chabreck, 1988). Especially large areas of marshes are found in the southern Atlantic states (North Carolina, South Carolina, and Georgia in particular) and the Gulf (Louisiana and Texas). Few coastal marshes are found in New

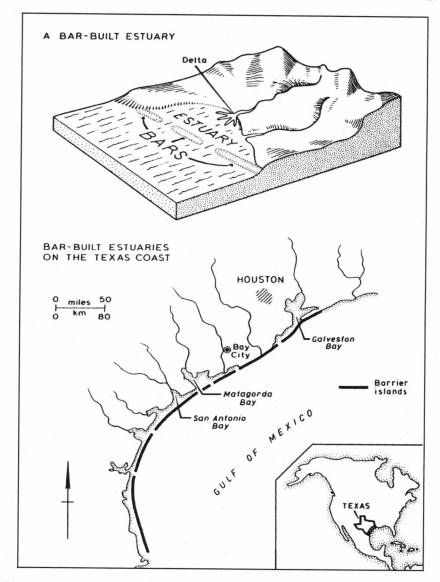

Figure 2.5   Bar-built estuaries on the Texas coast. (From Petrick, 1984.)

England or along the Pacific coast because of the rockier nature of these shorelines, though some are found in protected bays and river mouths. There are only an estimated 144 square miles of coastal marshes on the Pacific coast with the majority of these being associated with the San Francisco Bay (Chabreck, 1988). Coastal marshes are generally classified according to their salinity regimes, with four types commonly identified: salt marshes, brackish marshes, intermediate marshes, and freshwater marshes. The majority of coastal marshes (some 70%) are salt marshes. Salinity levels in turn influence the types of vegetation found in marshes, with some plant species, such as mangroves and cordgrass, very resistant to high saline levels, and other species, such as sawgrass or water hyacinth, not very suited to saline water conditions. Coastal types tend to occur in bands paralleling the coastline, consistent with salinity patterns.

Coastal marshes have been heavily modified by the human species. It is estimated that fewer than 50% of the coastal marshes that existed when the nation was first settled still remain (see Tiner, 1984). Marshes have been destroyed or damaged by a variety of activities, including conversion of land to agricultural production, filling for coastal homesites and development, and construction of canal dredging, among others. In coastal Louisiana, marshes have been disappearing largely as a result of extensive river diversion and flood control levee building. Because the marshlands of the Mississippi delta naturally subside, these flood control projects have deprived the marshes of the needed replacement sediment, and thus the wetlands are literally drowning. Because of the extensive levee and channelization project, the Mississippi River now deposits its sediments right off the edge of the continental shelf, in turn losing the material from the coastal system. It has been estimated that Louisiana loses some 40 square miles of marshes each year (Chabreck, 1988). Extensive canal dredging along the Gulf, for navigation and oil and gas production activities, has also been a major cause of marsh degradation as well as gradual saltwater intrusion.

Sea level rise in many ways represents the most serious current threat to marshes. Discussed in more detail below, increases in sea level rise threaten to inundate these productive areas faster than they can migrate landward (see Titus, 1991; Reid and Trexler, 1991).

Coastal marshlands are extremely ecologically productive and serve a number of important biological and human functions. They are an important food source for fish and shellfish, are home to a variety of wildlife, are important recreational areas, help reduce shoreline erosion and serve as natural flood mitigation devices (acting as natural sponges), and can provide natural wastewater and pollution treatment, among other benefits.

Coral Reefs

Coral reefs represent one of the earth's most ecologically productive habitats. Globally, coral reefs comprise about 600,000 square miles and support at least a half a million species of life. The net productivity of coral systems is actually higher than many tropical forests. While extremely productive, living coral systems are limited in the United States, with the most extensive system along the Florida Keys. Threats to coral reef systems are numerous and include harvesting of coral, blast fishing, damage from overuse by snorklers and divers, damage from ships, and sedimentation and water pollution. In the Caribbean, coral bleaching has been a concern in recent years and is seen by many as indicative of the level of stress placed on these living systems. Global climate change, and the resultant sea level rise and rises in seawater temperatures, could have a major damaging effect on the world coral reef systems. For instance, abnormally high water temperatures in the Caribbean is believed to be a major cause of recent bleaching episodes.

Renewed efforts are underway to protect coral reefs in the United States and elsewhere. For example, the U.S. Congress recently created a new large Florida Keys Marine Sanctuary, consolidating several pre-existing sanctuaries with the promise of more stringent control of damaging impacts, including nonpoint water pollutants.

The Dynamic Coastal Environment: Important Coastal Forces and Processes

Coastal areas clearly represent dynamic environments, where landforms are created and modified over time in response to inputs of energy and materials. Energy inputs include waves, tides, and wind.

Coastal materials are injected into this dynamic system in several ways, including deposition by rivers, wave-induced erosion, through biological generation (e.g., as through coral-type animals), and pre-existing off-shore sediment deposits.

Energy inputs manifest themselves in a number of important coastal processes, including the longshore transport of coastal materials and aerial sand transport. Hurricanes and coastal storms, as well as sea level rise, also are major players in modifying coastal landforms. These and other processes are described in more detail below.

It is important to again remember that these more immediate physical dynamics occur within a larger, and more stable, geologic context. Rocky coasts, which are higher and steeper, are generally less susceptible to the impacts of small changes in sea level rise than more depositional environments such as barrier island systems, for instance.

Wind, Waves, and Sediment Transport

The changing coastal ecosystem is very much the result of complex interactions among wind, waves, and materials. Accretion and erosion patterns on beaches and barrier islands, for instance, depend on a number of factors, including a complex sand transport system. Sand materials are obtained from several sources in nature, including terrestrial sources (e.g., materials made available through runoff and river transport), erosion of headlands and bluffs, biogenic production, and the inner continental shelf (National Research Council, 1990).

Wave conditions have a significant influence on sand transport and vary seasonally. An important factor is wave steepness (technically defined as the ratio of wave height to wave length). Steeper waves—waves with large height and short periods—are generally associated with stormy winter months, as well as hurricanes, and tend to cause beach erosion, which is reversed during summer months when the waves are milder and of a larger period. These seasonal changes in wave characteristics in turn result in seasonal changes in the width of beaches (i.e., beaches tend to be wider in the summer months and narrower in winter).

The coastal wave system also gives rise to the so-called longshore current (sometimes referred to as *littoral drift*). Because in many parts of the coastline waves approach the shore at oblique angles, sand materials are continually moved from updrift locations to downdrift locations. Problems often arise with the construction of groins and jetties, which interfere with this natural current. Without some mechanism for a sand-by, jetty construction serves to deprive down-coast locations of their natural flow of sand, in turn causing or exacerbating shoreline erosion there (this problem is discussed in greater detail in the following chapter).

Hurricanes and Coastal Storms

Hurricanes and coastal storms are a normal part of the coastal environment and are also major actors in modifying coastal landforms and ecosystems. As population and growth pressures along coastlines continue to rise, these large storm events represent a major threat to people and property.

Along the Gulf and Atlantic coasts, hurricanes and tropical storms represent a major threat. Hurricanes are cyclonic events with sustained wind speeds of at least 74 mph. On average, three hurricanes strike the coast every three years. The probability of being hit by a hurricane or tropical storm is not uniform but varies geographically (see Figure 2.6). As might be expected, certain states are more exposed and have received a greater number of hits. Florida has received the greatest number of hurricane landfalls, followed by Texas, Louisiana, and North Carolina.

The intensity and magnitude of hurricanes is evaluated on the Saffir/Simpson scale, which ranges from Category 1, the weakest, least-damaging hurricane, to Category 5, the most damaging (see Table 2.1).

In addition to hurricanes and tropical storms, East coast states are also subject to potentially devastating northeasters—storms which track down the coastline from the northeast. In fact, they are often more damaging because they often linger and batter coastlines for days at a time. (A new index—the Dolan/Davis index—of northeaster intensity has recently been developed.) While the Pacific coast states (with the exception of Hawaii) do not experience hurricanes or tropical storms, these coastlines do experience similarly severe storm events.

Forces associated with hurricanes and coastal storms include surge, heightened wave action, and high winds. Along the Gulf and Atlantic coasts, storm surges can be especially great as a result of the wider continental shelf and gently sloping shoreline. During Hurricane Hugo, for instance, storm surges at Bulls Bay, South Carolina, were as high as 20 feet above normal tides.

Storm flooding can result in substantial shoreline erosion and over-washing of barrier islands and, in certain instances, can cause breaches,

TABLE 2.1
Saffir/Simpson Hurricane Scale

Category	Winds (mph)	Surge (ft)	Central pressure (in.)	Damage	Example
1	74–95	4–5	≥ 28.94	Minimal	Cindy (1959)
2	96–110	6–8	28.50–28.91	Moderate	11 Aug. (1940)
3	111–130	9–12	27.91–28.47	Extensive	Gracie (1959)
4	131–155	13–18	27.17–27.88	Extreme	Hazel (1954)
5	>155	>18	< 27.17	Catastrophic	Prehistoric

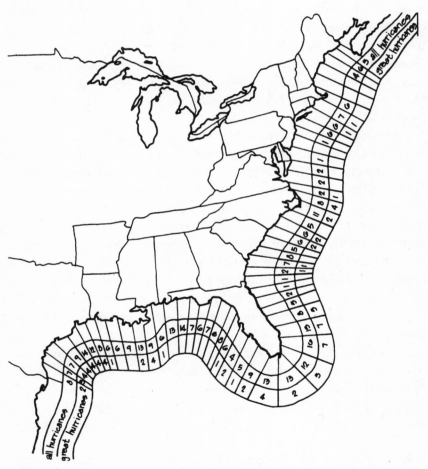

Figure 2.6 Hurricane experience of eastern United States, 1886–1970. (From FEMA, 1986.)

creating new inlets or reopening historical inlets. For example, a new inlet was formed on Pawleys Island, South Carolina, as a result of Hurricane Hugo. Storms take sand offshore, depositing it in sand bars, with much of it gradually returning later to the beach.

In addition to loss of human life and property damage, hurricanes and coastal storms can wreak substantial damage to the natural environment. Hurricane Hugo, for instance, did tremendous damage to the Francis Marion National Forest, destroying a high percentage of large-diameter pines. The storm also dealt a major negative blow to what had been one of the largest populations of the endangered red-cockaded woodpecker. Recently, Hurricane Iniki dealt a major blow to endangered plant and bird life on the island of Kauai.

Sea Level Rise

Over geologic time the rise and fall of the sea has been a major force in shaping coastlines. The last major period of sea level rise began approximately 18,000 years ago, at the end of the Pleistocene period (see Figure 2.7), and is, as already mentioned, a likely explanation for the U.S. barrier island system and for much of the shoreline retreat which has occurred around the world. While sea level rise slowed dramatically some 7,000 years ago, sea levels have been gradually rising over the last century, as measured through tidal gauges around the world. This recent historical rate has been on the order of about 1 to 2 millimeters per year, or about a foot per century. Even very small amounts of sea level rise, it should be remembered, can represent significant shoreline movement in low-lying and gradually sloping coastal areas such as along the East coast of the United States. It has been estimated that along gently sloping coastlines, landward or horizontal shoreline movement may be a thousand times greater than vertical sea level rise (e.g., for every foot of vertical sea level rise 1,000 feet of shoreline retreat may be experienced).

Largely in response to global warming, there has been considerable concern in recent years with the possibility of accelerated sea level rise. Global warming can cause sea levels to rise primarily for two reasons—thermal expansion and glacial melting. While there is not complete consensus among the scientific community about the realities of global warming, most agree that it is a real phenomenon. Much of the scientific disagreement recently has tended to center on the rate and

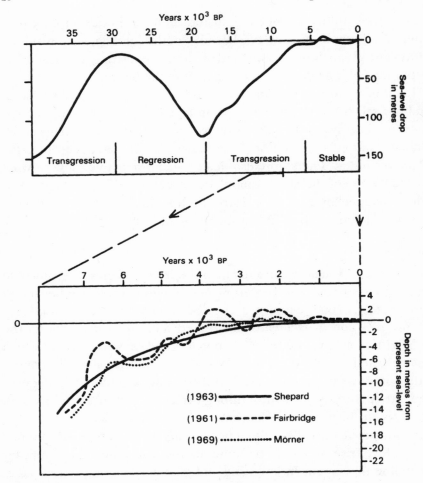

Figure 2.7   Sea level fluctuations in the last 35,000 years before present (BP). The curve in the upper diagram is based on only limited data, whereas the lower curves show that considerable disagreement exists over the position of sea levels during the last 7,000 years or so. Increasingly it is recognized that single global sea level curves like these may be unrealistic in view of the likelihood of local and regional tectonic coastal changes affecting sea level position. (From Hansom, 1988.)

degree of future global warming, and not on whether it will happen. The Intergovernmental Panel on Climate Change (IPCC), for instance, recently issued the findings of its scientific committee, which concluded that mean global temperature will likely rise by about 3°C before the end of the next century (their "best guess"; see Houghton et al., 1990).

Estimates of likely future sea level rise have varied considerably, but consensus seems to be developing around a likely range of 0.5 to 2 meters by the year 2100. Accelerated sea level rise could result in substantial flooding and inundation of both the built and the natural environments. Substantial property damage could result, and the U.S. Environmental Protection Agency (EPA) has sponsored several studies of the possible economic impacts of different sea level rise scenarios. In an analysis of the potential impacts in the Charleston, South Carolina area, Barth et al. (1984) predicted that by the year 2075 the region (including all of Charleston, parts of North Charleston, Mt. Pleasant, Sullivans Island, and James Island) would lose about 46% of its land area due to shoreline retreat under a high scenario and even about 30% under a medium scenario. (The high scenario assumed a 231.6-centimeter [7.6-foot] rise, and the medium scenario a 159.2-centimeter [5.2-foot] rise.) Under even the medium scenario some 60% of the region, by the year 2075, would be located within the 10-year floodplain and thus subject to substantial periodic flooding (assuming no collective response, such as building additional seawalls). Estimates of the economic impacts of these shoreline changes for the years 1980 through 2075 exceed $2.5 billion for the high scenario and nearly $2 billion under the medium scenario (Barth et al., 1984).

Reid and Trexler (1991) have undertaken an analysis of the potential impacts of sea level rise on coastal biodiversity. Coastal areas harbor a disproportionate number of rare and endangered species, and many of these are found only in a narrow band along the coast. More specifically, while the average number of federally listed species (endangered or threatened) found in counties in the continental United States is three to four, coastal counties on average contain many more. (Close to half of the coastal counties contain 10 to 20 listed species; see Flather and Hoekstra, 1989). Some 41 federally listed species, and another 128 candidate species, are found below the 10-foot elevation contour, with many completely restricted to these areas. These species range from the Key deer to the Perdido Key beach mouse, the California clapper rail, and the loggerhead sea turtle. Using The Nature Conservancy's designations of rare, imperiled, or critically imperiled, the number of species at risk and threatened with local extirpation jumps to 461 (with a large percentage of these species located in Florida). (See Table 2.2.)

TABLE 2.2
*Federal Threatened and Endangered Species and
State Rare Species in Coastal Regions.*

State[a]	Birds	Mammals	Reptiles/ amphibians	Fish	Plants	Total
I. Federally listed (endangered, threatened) species found within 10 feet of sea level (candidate species in parentheses)						
Oregon	4(2)	0	0	0	(2)	4(4)
Massachusetts	0	0	0	0	0	0
Maryland	2	1[1]	0	0	1(12)	4(12)
North Carolina	1	0	1	0	(7)	2(7)
Florida	8[2](5[2])	8[7](9[7])	9(9[3])	1(2[1])	12[1](83[14])	38(108)
II. Rare species restricted to within 5 feet of sea level						
Oregon	0	0	0	0	3[2]	3
Massachusetts	11	0	0	0	9[1]	20
Maryland	11	0	0	0	38	49
North Carolina	0	0	1	0	10	11
Florida	19[3]	11[9]	11[4]	2[1]	27[4]	70
III. Rare species found within 10 feet of sea level						
Oregon	7[1]	0	1	0	8	16
Massachusetts	17	1	1	1	22[1]	42
Maryland	16	1[1]	2	1	102[2]	122
North Carolina	1	0	1	0	19	21
Florida	35[8]	19[15]	30[14]	9[1]	167[18]	258

Source: Reid and Trexler (1991).

[a] State totals refer to the number of species determined by The Nature Conservancy to be "Critically Imperiled," "Imperiled," or "Rare or Uncommon" in that state. A species may be common in other states and still be listed if rare in the particular state. Superscript indicates the number of subspecies (or varieties) included in the total.

Many of these species depend upon coastal wetland habitats, and there have been several analyses of the potential loss in wetlands that could result from future sea level rise. Park et al. (1989), for instance, undertook an analysis of three different scenarios of possible sea level rise by the year 2010: a 50-, 100-, and 200-centimeter rise. The study also assumed different levels of human response to sea level rise (protection of all dryland through dikes and levees; protection only of areas already served by dikes and levees). The high scenarios result in the most dramatic results, with 61–70% of coastal wetlands being lost with a 2-meter rise in sea level. Under the medium scenario of a 1-meter rise, 46–52% of coastal wetlands are lost. Even under the low scenario, where all land is assumed protected with dikes and levees, wetland loss is as high as 26%. Other estimates of future wetland loss resulting from sea level rise have produced similar results (e.g., see Titus, 1991).

Coastal Hydrologic Cycle

Also critical to understanding the coastal ecosystem is knowledge of the hydrologic cycle. Many components of this system have already been discussed (e.g., under Estuaries), but a brief description of the larger system is appropriate. As already described, estuarine systems are characterized by the interaction and influx of ocean waters and freshwaters. The flow of freshwater toward the sea is a function of the characteristics of the drainage basin and the flow of surface waters (e.g., creeks, streams, rivers) as well as groundwater contributions. The water budget is in turn heavily determined by rates of precipitation and evapotranspiration (see Clark 1977). Precipitation contributes to surface waters through runoff and to groundwater aquifers through percolation and infiltration (see Figure 2.8).

Groundwater resources are important in coastal regions and are a major source of drinking water and water for industrial and commercial activities. On barrier islands a small lens of groundwater is typically found, which is easily exhausted and overdrawn. On barrier islands, as well as on other elements of the coastal environment, heavy withdrawal of groundwater has resulted in problems of saltwater intrusion. Future sea level rise may also exacerbate saltwater intrusion problems by extending landward the saltwater wedge.

Conclusions

This chapter has provided a general introduction to the physical characteristics and natural processes present in the coastal environment. This environment is highly dynamic and also very ecologically productive. While the reader is encouraged to look elsewhere for detailed scientific discussions of these issues, it is clear that any attempt

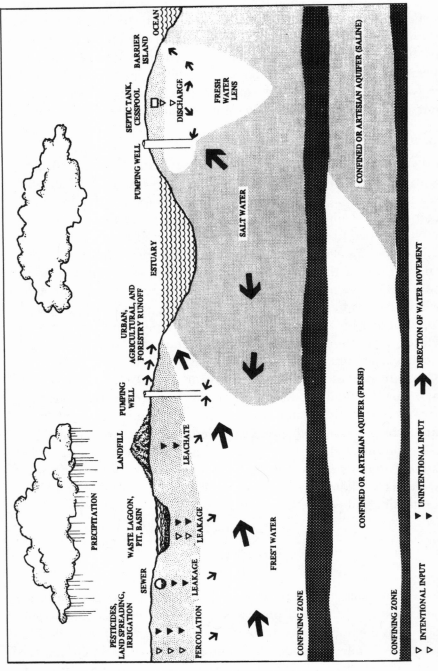

Figure 2.8 The groundwater–estuarine connection and sources of pollution. (From North Carolina Division of Coastal Management, 1988.)

at coastal management must begin with an understanding of the coastal environment; an understanding, for instance, that barrier islands are subject to a host of natural forces and dynamics. This suggests special care concerning where and how to build in these areas to minimize negative impacts on the ecosystem and to reduce exposure of people and property to unnecessary risks such as shoreline erosion, hurricanes, and other manifestations of the forces of nature.

3

Coastal Pressures and Critical Management Issues

The Coastal Nation

Demographic trends suggest that coastal areas around the world, including those in the United States, are undergoing serious population growth pressures. Already, in the United States nearly half of the country's population resides in coastal counties. The growth of coastal areas has been dramatic and projections continue to suggest that coastal areas will grow rapidly. Culliton et al. (1990) predicts that by the year 2010, the coastal population will grow to 127 million (see Figure 3.1). This represents a 60% increase from the coastal population in 1960. During this period the population of Florida will have grown from 5 million to 16 million, an increase greater than three-fold over a 50-year period. Of the 20 states expected to have the largest growth rates over the next 30 years, 17 are coastal (Culliton et al., 1991; see also Reid and Trexler, 1991). Between 1960 and 2010, Florida is the coastal state expected to have grown in population by the largest percentage, by some 226%, followed by Alaska, New Hampshire, California, and Texas (see Table 3.1; from Culliton et al., 1991). California is expected to experience the largest absolute growth among coastal states, followed by Texas, Florida, Georgia, and Virginia.

Certain coastal counties are projected to be very high-growth jurisdictions. For example, the southern California counties (Los Angeles, Orange, and San Diego) and the counties around Miami (Dade, Broward, and Palm Beach) are expected to experience very high amounts of growth. Regionally, the largest coastal populations are found in the Northeast and the Pacific regions, together comprising about 30% of the total U.S. population.

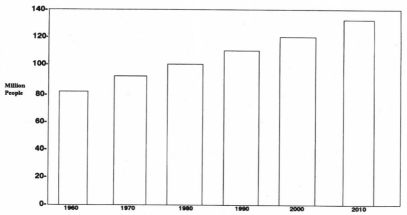

Figure 3.1 Population growth projections for coastal U.S. counties. (From Culliton et al., 1991.)

Table 3.1

Leading Coastal States in Population Change, 1960–2010

State	Absolute[a]	State	Percentage
California	19.2	Florida	226
Texas	11.6	Alaska	208
Florida	11.2	New Hampshire	129
Georgia	3.5	California	122
Virginia	3.0	Texas	121

Source: Culliton et al. (1991).
[a]Million persons.

Population density is another measure of the stresses placed on coastal areas. Even in 1960, coastal population densities were much higher than other parts of the country. In that year the average population density for the nation as a whole was 62 persons per square mile, compared with 248 persons per square mile in coastal counties. This coastal population density was up to 341 persons per square mile by 1988, some 4 times the national average (see Figure 3.2).

Some statistics are also available on the extent to which the U.S. population is utilizing coastal areas for recreational purposes. National Park Service data suggests that visitation to national parks, national seashores, and national monuments has risen markedly in recent years. Between 1979 and 1988, visitation at these park units has risen by 63% (and 78% for the 10 national seashores) (Culliton et al., 1991).

Land Use Patterns and Human Alterations of the Coastal Zone

Historically, and for obvious reasons, settlement of the United States began along its coastlines. Since these early settlement days the U.S. coastline has been utilized in a number of ways. Largely for transportation reasons, major industrial and commercial centers developed around port cities. Cities such as Norfolk, Virginia, and Seattle, Washington, remain important ports. In more recent decades (as the above statistics indicate), uses of the coastline have shifted to include substantial recreational and conservation uses. Recreational and resort developments have substantially increased in recent history.

Resource uses of the coastal zone remain significant, including agricultural and fishing industries, and the more recent oil, gas, and minerals extraction.

These human uses of the U.S. coastline have caused considerable damage to the coastal environment in a number of ways. Historically, development has resulted in the destruction of wetlands, the leveling of dunes, and the degradation of water quality, among other impacts. Moreover, the natural coastal environment has in many areas been replaced with a heavily human-managed landscape, through the construction of seawalls and revetments, groins and jetties, and dams and other flood control projects. These issues are described in more detail below.

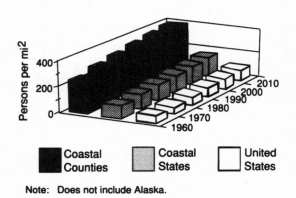

Note: Does not include Alaska.

Figure 3.2   Population density, 1960–2010. (From Culliton et al., 1991.)

Patterns of Ownership and Control

The U.S. coastal zone represents a complex pattern of ownership and control. As Figure 3.3 indicates, there are several important jurisdictional zones extending seaward from the land. Seaward of mean high water (MHW) is the territorial sea, which originally, under international law, was measured by the distance of a cannon shot. In the United States it was three miles from MHW, and this area was given to the states by Congress under the terms of the Submerged Lands Act of 1953. The Convention on the Territorial Sea and Contiguous Zone of 1958 allows a country to claim a contiguous zone beyond the territorial sea up to 12 miles. In 1988 President Reagan extended the territorial sea to 12 miles by proclamation, but this did not generally extend the states' rights, although Texas and Florida have established claims beyond three miles. In 1976 Congress passed the Fishery Conservation and Management Act (the Magnuson Act), extending an exclusive fishery conservation zone to 200 miles, and in 1983 President Reagan proclaimed a 200-mile Exclusive Economic Zone (EEZ). Beyond the EEZ are the high seas, in which no nation can assert sovereignty.

As coastal states become increasingly involved in ocean management it is likely that they will seek to extend their control and management beyond the existing territorial limit. The state of Oregon, for instance, under its Ocean Resources Management Program, has

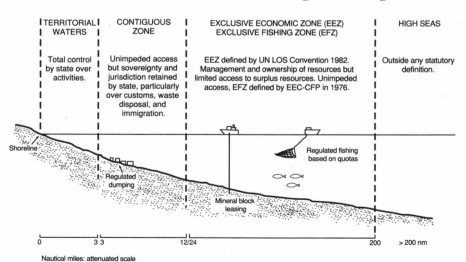

Figure 3.3   Cross-shore and cross-shelf judicial and legislative zones. Note that 1 nautical mile equals 1.85 km. (From Carter, 1990.)

proposed the establishment of an Ocean Stewardship Area, which would extend seaward to the base of the continental margin (extending from 35 to 80 miles seaward), and in which their management and planning activities would be focused. At least for purposes of planning coordination, coastal states are increasingly likely, then, to want to expand their influence beyond the 12-mile limit.

Layered on top of these zones are additional rights of public use and access created through a combination of federal and state laws, constitutions, and judicial interpretations. Under the federal doctrine of navigational servitude, the federal government protects the right of access and movement along navigable waters, and exercises regulatory control over structures and activities that may impede this right.

At the state level, common law doctrine has played an important role in establishing public rights of access to coastal resources. In a majority of coastal states the public trust doctrine (or a similar doctrinal basis) ensures the public's right to walk along and utilize the shoreline (or a certain portion of it). The boundary of this public right varies from state to state, but seaward of mean high water is the typical boundary, thus protecting access to the wet beach.

In some states, notably Texas and Oregon, the public trust boundary is the first natural line of vegetation, thus encompassing a sizable portion of the dry beach as well. This line of demarcation has been interpreted through the courts to be dynamic and subject to periodic movement, as in response to natural erosion or coastal storms. Thus the line is a sort of "rolling public easement" with considerable implication for coastal homeowners. A major example of these implications occurred following Hurricane Alicia, which struck the Galveston, Texas, shoreline in 1983 (Godschalk et al., 1989). Because the first line of vegetation was moved landward by the hurricane, buildings that were once landward of this line were then located seaward following the storm. Homeowners with heavily damaged structures were prevented from rebuilding by the state, because such reconstruction would then have been located on the public beach. Several landowners sued the state, claiming the restrictions amounted to unconstitutional takings by the state. The state supreme court, however, found in favor of the state, upholding the public's ownership of the dry beach, under the doctrine of customary use.

Each coastal state engaging in some degree of coastal zone management will also have delimited certain regulatory zones, in which

certain permits are required and to which certain performance standards are mandated before development or use of these areas can proceed. Under the 1988 South Carolina Beachfront Management Act, for
instance, a series of regulatory lines were delimited, including a base-
line (crest of ideal dune), a no-construction line, and a 40-year erosion
setback line. Under the original 1988 act (since modified), new habitable structures were prohibited seaward of the no-construction zone
(the so-called "dead zone"), and structures within the 40-year setback
zone could be no larger than 5,000 square feet in size. A series of other
restrictions applied to these zones as well, including restrictions on rebuilding in the event of hurricane or storm damages (e.g., see Beatley,
1992).

Actual ownership patterns along the coast are a mixture of public and
private. Public ownership occurs, to some extent, at all governmental
levels. At the federal level, ownership of conservation units consists of
national seashores (such as Cape Hatteras National Seashore), national
recreation areas (such as the Oregon Dunes National Recreational
Area), national wildlife refuges (such as the Alligator River National
Wildlife Refuge), national monuments, and national forests (such as
the Francis Marion National Forest on the South Carolina coast).
Extensive federal military facilities also exist (e.g., Cherry Point Naval
Air Station, Camp Pendleton Marine Base, etc.).

Planning and management of these different federal units is splin-
tered. For example, the U.S. Fish and Wildlife Service has authority
over national wildlife refuges, while the National Park Service has control over national seashores and monuments. The U.S. Forest Service,
on the other hand, has authority over the management of national
forests.

State ownership includes state parks, wildlife management areas,
and state historic sites. Extensive local ownership of coastal lands is
less typical. However, it is not uncommon for coastal localities to own
beachfront parks and recreational facilities. The city of Myrtle Beach,
South Carolina, for instance, owns a major strip of beachfront land.

Critical Coastal Management Issues

The population and development pressures that many coastal areas
have been experiencing in turn generate a number of potential problems and policy issues. What follows is a brief listing/identification of

some of the more critical of these contemporary management issues facing America's coastal areas and a discussion of some of the policy and planning options available to address them.

Coastal Storm Mitigation

As discussed in Chapter 2, the U.S. coastline is subject to a variety of coastal storm threats. Along the Gulf and Atlantic coasts, hurricanes and tropical storms are a normal and regular occurrence. While the chances of any one location being struck are fairly small, the physical forces are severe and the impacts potentially catastrophic, forcing coastal states and localities to resolve with how best to cope with these threats. In addition to hurricanes, the East coast faces a severe northeaster threat, and the Pacific coast and other parts of the U.S. coastline face similar storm threats.

Hurricanes have the capability of causing major loss of life and property destruction. The Galveston Island hurricane of 1900 resulted in some 6,000 deaths. Because of the development of a reliable hurricane tracking and warning system in the United States, the number of deaths from hurricanes has gradually been on the decline over the last century. The trend for property destruction, however, has been in the other direction, markedly on the rise. The astronomical property damage wrought by Hurricane Andrew—perhaps on the order of $20 billion—illustrates the vulnerability of public and private property along the coastline and the likely future direction of property damage trends. The threat from hurricanes and other coastal storms has increased substantially due to coastal population trends, since the amount of property and people now living in high-risk coastal zones has risen dramatically. Much of this development and growth has occurred since the 1950s and during an unusual lull in major storm activity. Only a relatively small percentage of the coastal population has actually experienced a hurricane or major storm; surveys show some 70% of the present coastal population has not.

To protect coastal property, states and localities have a number of different policy options. Discussed in greater detail in later chapters, these options include, among others,

- structural reinforcement (e.g., seawalls)

- "soft" shoreline reinforcement (beach renourishment)
- hazard zone avoidance (e.g., coastal setbacks, density restrictions)
- building codes and elevation

A major policy distinction can be made between strategies which seek to avoid exposure (e.g., keeping buildings out of high-risk coastal hazard zones) and those which seek to buttress against the forces of nature (e.g., seawalls).

Evacuation is also a major policy issue in most coastal areas, especially on barrier island communities, where population growth has resulted in substantial increases in the time it takes to evacuate residents in the event of an oncoming storm. On Galveston Island, Texas, for instance, evacuation times are estimated at between 24 and 36 hours, and rising. Substantial rises in evacuation times can be seen in the Outer Banks of North Carolina and the Florida Keys, among many other coastal locations. Moreover, most hurricane experts admit that we have reached a plateau in the ability to predict the future direction of a hurricane and to warn coastal communities of an oncoming storm. The National Hurricane Center in Coral Gables, Florida, is very good at tracking hurricanes, but the unpredictable nature of these events means that they often do not go where they are expected to go. Hurricane Elena is a case in point. The tracking map for this event illustrates how unpredictable hurricanes can be, changing directions and speed several times, and largely confounding predictions about its likely landfall. Thus, while the National Hurricane Center says it can provide approximately 12 hours of quality warning time (prior to a strike), evacuation times in many communities are much longer. This frequently presents the dilemma for coastal officials who must decide to call for an evacuation many hours prior to knowing whether the storm will actually strike their location.

In planning for evacuation, coastal states and communities have many options, including

- horizontal evacuation (building a sufficient bridge and road infrastructure to allow evacuation; maintaining adequate warning and preparedness systems, etc.)
- vertical evacuation (housing a significant number of coastal residents in engineered structures during a storm event)

• growth caps (e.g., limit the amount of development permissible in
  order not to exceed a certain evacuation capability, such as the approach taken by Sanibel Island, Florida)

Vertical evacuation has so far not been heavily utilized in coastal
areas. However, the feeling of many experts is that in those areas
where population and development continue to explode, this approach may in fact be the only option available. There are a number of
potential difficulties in vertical evacuation. One is simply finding engineered structures that can be assured of surviving during a hurricane
or major storm event. However, recent structural surveys are discouraging on this point, indicating that few buildings are safe enough to
serve as shelters during a storm. Potential legal liability is another possible limitation which has not yet been completely resolved. Some
critics of vertical evacuation have charged that its use may serve as a
way to justify even greater development and growth in coastal areas
(Salmon, 1984).

Shoreline Erosion and Sea Level Rise

While hurricanes are infrequent yet catastrophic events, many coastal
areas are facing long-term shoreline erosion problems. This is especially a problem along the low-lying barrier island systems of the Gulf
and Atlantic coasts. While some coastal areas may be accreting in the
short term, the general trend is in the direction of shoreline retreat.
Historically, the U.S. barrier island system has been gradually moving
landward, largely in response to gradual sea level rise (Pilkey et al.,
1980; Kaufman and Pilkey, 1979).

Few national assessments of the shoreline erosion problem have
been undertaken. One of the few, a 1971 Corps of Engineers study,
found that about 40% of the U.S. coastline was experiencing "significant erosion," with another 7% experiencing "critical erosion" (Platt,
1991; NRC, 1990).

A variety of other human alterations can affect shoreline erosion and
accretion patterns. The construction of jetties and groins can serve to
interrupt normal littoral drift, depriving down-coast areas of sand sediment and causing erosion. One of the places where this impact has
been most dramatic is in Ocean City, Maryland. Here, a jetty system
was constructed to keep the Ocean City inlet open. The jetty on

Fenwick Island (the Ocean City side) has severely interrupted sand movement to Assateauge Island to the south, causing severe erosion there. Construction of seawalls and revetments has also been found to exacerbate shoreline erosion by reflecting wave energy and steepening offshore profiles (Pilkey, 1989).

The damming and diverting of rivers has also caused erosion by depriving coastal areas of important fluvial sediment. This is most dramatic in coastal Louisiana, where extensive wetlands are subsiding and disappearing because of the diversion of replacement sediments from the Mississippi River. Another example is found in the Santee River delta in South Carolina.

Global warming, or the so-called "greenhouse effect," has the potential to cause significant accelerated sea level rise, as described in Chapter 2, with even greater levels of shoreline erosion and retreat predicted. As described earlier, predicted levels would result in the inundation of coastal communities such as Charleston, South Carolina, and Galveston Island, Texas, causing considerable property damage. Sea level rise would also result in major flooding and destruction of coastal wetlands, as well as other negative impacts on the coastal environment (e.g., exacerbating saltwater intrusion; see generally Edgerton, 1991).

Policy options available to coastal states and localities in dealing with these issues are several and have already been mentioned. At a fundamental level, coastal jurisdictions can choose either to *resist* or to *battle* these coastal forces (e.g., by reinforcing the coastline through seawalls and other coastal works) or they can choose to engage in *strategic retreat* from the shoreline. These options are described in greater detail in the following section.

Long-term shoreline erosion and sea level rise represent major future challenges for coastal states and localities to deal with. So far, while a number of states and localities have adopted some measures to address erosion (e.g., coastal setbacks), few have explicitly incorporated potential sea level rise effects into their planning and policies (Brower and Stevens, 1992), although states are clearly beginning to think about the issue (see Klarin and Hershman, 1990).

It is frequently argued that federal programs and subsidies have served to encourage risky patterns of development along coastlines. It can be argued that the federal government has created a system of "perverse" incentives which have actually encouraged dangerous and irrational building patterns. These subsidies have included federal flood insurance, disaster assistance, and casualty loss deductions under the federal income tax code. These programs will be taken up again and discussed in more detail in subsequent chapters.

Strategic Retreat or Coastal Reinforcement

Given the forces of long-term erosion, hurricanes and coastal storms, and sea level rise, some argue that a policy of "strategic retreat" is in order. State and local setback restrictions, restrictions on rebuilding following storms, and programs and policies to promote landward relocation can all promote retreat. Some coastal management programs, such as New York's erosion management law, prevent the construction of "immovable" structures in high-erosion zones. Some proponents of strategic retreat believe that if a building or improvement cannot be moved, it should be allowed to fall into the ocean.

Such positions are obviously controversial, and not well received by coastal homeowners and local government officials. They argue that such a radical retreat policy ignores the large amount of public and private property at risk and the inefficiency of not protecting it from the forces of nature. Several options for protecting public and private property are advocated, for example, structural approaches, including construction of seawalls and revetments, groins and jetties, offshore breakwaters, and other shore-armoring devices. While these devices may temporarily block flooding and erosion, their economic and environmental impacts are substantial. Continuing seawalls can exacerbate erosion, block normal landward migration of barrier islands, and eventually result in a highly engineered shoreline with no natural beach. This is a process described by Pilkey as "New Jersization" of the shoreline (Pilkey et al., 1980).

An increasingly popular middle ground solution is beach renourishment or replenishment. Here, typically off-shore sand deposits are dredged and pumped onto eroding beaches. Beach renourishment can restore the recreational beach and protect (to some extent) shoreline structures from erosion and storm forces. However, recent studies of beach renourishment projects suggest that the practice is very expensive and relatively short-lived. Estimates of the time periods renourishment will last before additional renourishing is necessary have been consistently over-estimated (especially by the U.S. Army Corps of Engineers, which carries out extensive beach renourishment projects). The strategy of renourishing commits a community to a never-ending and expensive process. It appears an especially defensible method in coastal communities, such as Virginia Beach, Virginia, and Ocean City, Maryland, where millions of dollars of property is at risk and where maintaining a recreational beach is necessary for generating extensive economic activities (i.e., beachfront hotels, boardwalk businesses).

Protection of Coastal Wetlands and Resourcelands

As observed in Chapter 2, loss of coastal wetlands has been a significant problem in the past. Indeed, nearly half of all coastal wetlands have been destroyed since pre-Columbian times. Threats to wetlands have included draining and filling for agriculture, road construction, and urban and recreational development. Degradation through non-point pollution remains a significant problem. In the future, sea level rise may represent the most serious long-term threat to wetlands, and sizable portions of coastal wetlands would be inundated even under moderate scenarios.

Losses of coastal wetlands have clearly slowed dramatically in the last two decades largely as a result of enactment of tougher federal and state coastal wetlands protection laws. At the federal level, wetlands are offered protection through Section 404 of the Clean Water Act. Most coastal states have themselves adopted coastal wetland protection laws, often stricter and more comprehensive than the federal provisions. Major large-scale projects of filling and draining of coastal marshes have mostly stopped.

However, the coastal wetlands picture is not completely a rosey one. Major losses continue to occur, for example, in Louisiana as a result of rapid land subsidence and diversion of the Mississippi River. While large-scale wetlands destruction has nearly stopped, destruction of wetlands, for roads, marinas, seawalls, etc., is still occurring through the existing regulatory framework. At the federal level, the Section 404 program contains significant implementation "loopholes," and recent efforts have been made by the current national administration to redefine what legally constitutes a wetland, reducing substantially the area over which federal permit control would exist. At the state level, moreover, while some states have stringent provisions, others, such as Texas, have essentially no control over private wetlands.

Federal and state wetlands programs, furthermore, typically do not forbid all development or use of wetlands, but merely place restrictions on the types of uses permitted and the conditions under which these uses can occur. One issue involves the notion of so-called "water-dependent" uses. Many state wetlands laws forbid destruction of wetlands for uses or activities which are not water-dependent. Such uses clearly include such things as marinas, but do they also include seafood restaurants wanting marshfront locations, or hotels or motels wanting to capitalize on impressive shoreline views? Wetlands destruction is also typically only allowed where no feasible or "practicable" alternative locations exist, raising similarly difficult interpretation questions.

While large-scale coastal wetlands loss is now uncommon there remains the problem of incremental and piecemeal losses and the concern that the wetlands resource base is slowly being "nickeled and dimed to death" (Reid and Miller, 1989). The cumulative ecological impact of these incremental wetlands losses is currently not well understood. Furthermore, in many states there is not even the capability or effort made to keep track of the number of acres lost each year or the quality of these losses. The state of Virginia, for instance, has only recently started to monitor and keep a running tally of these losses (e.g., see Institute for Environmental Negotiation, 1991).

When applicants are permitted to fill or otherwise destroy natural wetlands, they are frequently required, either through the federal 404 program or state laws, to "mitigate" for these losses. Often this mitigation takes the form of requiring the applicant to compensate for or replace the wetlands with newly created wetlands or restoration of degraded wetlands. This remains a controversial practice and a number of recent studies raise serious questions about the efficacy of such practices (see Zedler, 1991, for an especially critical appraisal of this practice).

Protection of Coastal Waters

Protection of coastal waters is a major goal of coastal management programs. Bays and estuaries and other coastal waters are subject to a variety of pollutants, both point and nonpoint sources. Historically, industrial point sources were a significant problem as factories and other manufacturing activities have located along water bodies. Not surprisingly, recent studies of the water quality in the waters around several major cities find high concentrations of pollutants in shellfish and other aquatic life and in sediments.

Nonpoint pollutants from agriculture are also a major problem, generating excessive levels of nutrients, especially nitrogen and phosphorous, which are found in fertilizers and animal manure. In the Chesapeake Bay, for example, excessive nutrient levels have resulted in high algal growth, clouding waters and reducing oxygen availability for aquatic life (Horton, 1991). Urban nonpoint sources include runoff from streets and roads and other impervious surfaces; leachate from septic tanks, which is also a major problem in coastal areas; and construction sites, which generate a substantial amount of sediment runoff.

States and localities have sought to control these and other nonpoint pollutants through best management practices (BMPs). Agricultural BMPs include contour plowing, crop rotation, filter strips, animal waste control, and retirement of highly erodible land. Urban BMPs include stormwater collection ponds, infiltration basins and swales, use of porous asphalt, and restrictions on impervious surfaces. Construction BMPs include phased land clearance, filter fencing, protection of trees and vegetation, grading restrictions, runoff diversions, and location and design of road beds, among others.

Some of the more promising approaches to controlling nonpoint pollutants involve maintaining, to the extent possible, the ameliorative capabilities of the coastal ecosystem. Maintaining natural forested lands along the shore's edge, for instance, helps to filter pollutants and to take up excess nutrients. A number of state and local coastal programs mandate shoreline buffers along rivers and waterbodies (e.g., Virginia's Chesapeake Bay Preservation Act). Maintaining as much unpaved land as possible, and placing restrictions on the percentage of land in development projects that is impervious (where percolation and infiltration of rainwater is not possible), will further reduce amounts of urban and rural runoff (Toner, et al., 1984).

While passage of the Clean Water Act in 1972, and subsequent reauthorizations, has done much to reduce major point sources, the nonpoint source problem has historically received much less attention.

Controlling nonpoint pollution is a major policy issue in most coastal areas, and in recent years there has been a considerable reemphasis on nonpoint sources. The most recent reauthorization of the federal Coastal Zone Management Act has as a major centerpiece the control of nonpoint pollutants, creating major new requirements in this area for coastal states.

Placing controls on agricultural activities is especially controversial in coastal areas, and agriculture, historically exempted from many environmental provisions, has been able to secure a sort of preferred status among land users. For coastal managers, putting into place effective controls on agricultural activities is a major challenge.

There has also been a major concern in recent years over the water quality impacts of oil and gas development and transport. Off-shore oil and gas development has become increasingly unpopular, especially in states like California and Florida, and recent new restrictions have been placed on these activities in these and other coastal states. The potential impact of oil spills is also a major concern, heightened by the *Exxon Valdez* spill resulting in the discharge of 11 million gallons of crude oil into the sensitive ecosystem of Prince William Sound. This spill led to significant new restrictions on tanker design and procedures (requirements for double hulls, for instance).

Biodiversity and Habitat Conservation

As noted in Chapter 2, coastal areas are home to tremendous biological diversity. While biodiversity refers to the diversity of species, it also refers to diversity within species and the diversity of broader ecological communities and processes. Coastal areas do very well on all measures of diversity (Reid and Miller, 1989; Reid and Trexler, 1991).

As Reid and Trexler (1991) noted, coastal jurisdictions contain a disproportionate number of rare and endangered species. Moreover, coastlines represent important habitat for numerous species that may not be endangered. Many forms of life rely entirely or partially upon coastal shorelines. A recent study by the Florida Game and Freshwater Fish Commission found that of the state's 668 taxa of native vertebrates, coastal habitats were of high relative importance for vulnerable taxa, particularly for reptiles, birds, and mammals (see Millsap et al., 1990).

As development of coastal areas continues, habitat loss remains as a significant problem. There are numerous examples of direct conflicts between demands for resort development, second homes, and other development proposals, and the habitat needs of an endangered species.

In the Florida Keys, the endangered Key deer is threatened by increasing development, automobile traffic (road kills are a major factor), and the gradual loss of habitat, as well as the interference of development with essential movement corridors. Along the California coast, the California gnatcatcher and other species indigenous to coastal sage scrub habitat are increasingly threatened. Along Virginia's coast, barrier coastal development (e.g., on Cedar Island) threatens the piping plover. Expanding shoreline development has taken away nesting sites for endangered sea turtles, and extensive "lighting" of coastlines has lead to serious disorienting of newly hatched turtles.

Efforts are underway to protect coastal biodiversity. In the United States many of these efforts have resulted directly from the stringent requirements of the federal Endangered Species Act (ESA), which generally prohibits the taking of listed species (except under certain limited circumstances). Species conservation efforts have occurred in the coastal zone, including, for instance, the preparation of habitat conservation plans (HCPs) which seek to balance development and conservation interests (e.g., see Beatley 1991). Recent trends have been in the direction of preparing "multiple species" plans and plans which seek to protect larger ecosystem units and broader patterns of diversity.

Land acquisition remains an important strategy for preserving coastal biodiversity, and has occurred through federal, state, and private means (e.g., The Nature Conservancy). The state of Florida, for example, has been a leader in acquiring and setting aside sensitive lands through its Conservation and Recreation Lands program. There is also a growing recognition that to ensure long-term ecological viability of protected lands, sufficient linkages and corridors must be provided. This is especially true for species such as the Florida panther that require relatively large blocks of habitat. As coastal development continues, habitat fragmentation remains a growing concern.

The Coast as a Recreational Commons: Protecting Access to Beaches and Shorelines

The coast is an immense recreational resource enjoyed by millions each year. Yet, as coastal growth and development continue, public access to the coastline or the beach may itself become difficult.

Substantial conflicts arise between the desires of coastal developers, resort owners, and private property owners to secure and protect shoreline locations, and the goal of ensuring public access to, and enjoyment of, coastal areas. As noted earlier, most state common law protects at least the right of the public to walk along the wet beach unimpeded. However, in many coastal areas a wall of private development exists, and actual access to the beach is quite limited.

Many parts of the coast have been developed, or are being developed, as restricted or "guard-gate" developments. Private barrier island developments, such as Hilton Head and Kiawah Islands, restrict shoreline access to property owners or guests. While the public may be entitled to visit and walk upon the beach, there may be no physical way to reach these areas (short of by boat). Should such private developments be able to essentially appropriate this collective resource? Should public beach access be required, as it is now in some states and localities, as a condition of development approval?

Other types of actions or policies can also serve to effectively restrict access. For instance, some beach communities impose fees or restrict parking for nonresidents, in turn reducing public access. Increasingly, coastal states are establishing certain minimum access requirements that localities must satisfy before they are eligible for certain types of state monies (e.g., state beach renourishment monies).

Private Property versus the Public Interest in Coastal Planning

One of the most significant policy dilemmas in contemporary coastal management is determining the appropriate balance between, on the one hand, government police power regulations of coastal lands to protect and promote the public interest and, on the other, the sanctity of private property. Very frequently coastal property owners affected by coastal regulations (e.g., coastal setbacks, restrictions on filling wetlands) claim that such regulations are unconstitutional, amounting to takings under the Fifth Amendment of the U.S. Constitution (as well as similar provisions in state constitutions).

The Takings Clause of the Fifth Amendment provides that "private property shall [not] be taken for public use, without just compensation." The Fifth Amendment does not deny the government proper exercise of its "police power." States and municipalities may regulate property and its uses, without the owner necessarily being entitled to compensation. The government's police power involves the power to legislate to further the health, morals, safety, or welfare of the community, even where that legislation imposes a burden on the use and enjoyment of private property. The difference between situations which involve eminent domain (a governmental taking of private property which requires monetary compensation to the owner) and those where there is a legitimate exercise of police power (where no compensation is due) has been described by Justice Holmes as one of *degree* (*Pennsylvania Coal Co. v. Mahon*, 260 U.S. 393 [1922]).

The courts have never articulated a clear and definitive set of criteria for determining when a taking has occurred, and different judicial approaches and theories have contributed to considerable confusion about how far restrictions on coastal development and land use can go.

A recent South Carolina case highlights the ethical and legal disagreements which arise over the so-called takings issue. David Lucas owned two beachfront lots in the Wild Dunes subdivision on Isle of Palms, a barrier island community east of Charleston. After he acquired the lots, the South Carolina legislature enacted the Beachfront Management Act, placing major new restrictions on beachfront building. As noted earlier, under this 1988 law, new construction was prohibited seaward of certain lines. Both of the Lucas lots were seaward of this point, and thus were unbuildable under the law. Lucas sued the South Carolina Coastal Council, claiming a taking had occurred. The trial court agreed and awarded Lucas $1.2 million. The Coastal Council appealed and won in the South Carolina Supreme Court, which concluded that the state was merely preventing a public harm and therefore compensation was not required. Lucas appealed this decision to the U.S. Supreme Court, which reversed and remanded. The Court reinforced the notion that where a regulation serves to preclude all reasonable economic use of land, a taking is likely to have occurred. The Court did, however, suggest that the constitutionality of certain regulations might preclude all economic use if all that the state or local regulations are doing is effecting a pre-existing common law restriction, in particular, the common law of nuisance.

The Lucas case highlights the centrality of the takings issue in coastal management—important in a legal, political, and philosophical sense. Key questions remain, including under what circumstances it can be said that all economic uses have been extinguished. In the

South Carolina case, for instance, Lucas still had the right to use his land, to erect a temporary structure, and to sell it to an adjoining landowner.

Social Equity in Coastal Planning

Social equity is also a major issue in contemporary coastal planning and management (and related to the earlier issue of beach access). Many recent coastal communities have tended to develop as upper-income resort or vacation communities. The result is that coastal land values frequently rise, displacing low- and moderate-income residents. Paradoxically, environmental regulations, beach access requirements, and other coastal management requirements are sometimes also accused of contributing to the high cost of living in coastal areas and, especially, to the high cost of housing. Over time, then, there has been a "gentrification" of the coastal zone.

In many coastal states there are now rather sharp spatial distinctions between newer and often quite exclusive beachfront resort communities and the surrounding rural communities. The latter areas (e.g., much of the rural coastal plain of North Carolina) are often quite poor and exhibit lower income and education levels and, generally, lower housing and living conditions. Debate sometimes centers around the extent to which these poorer surrounding communities actually benefit economically from recent coastal development, and whether these spatial inequalities represent a major social injustice. While poorer residents are valued as service workers, it is often difficult for them to locate affordable housing (if it exists at all) in these resort communities. Mobile homes are a major source of affordable housing but are often prohibited or severely restricted in resort communities. Provision of affordable housing is in general a major policy issue which must be confronted in the coastal zone.

Displacement of poor and minority residents by new coastal development has also been a major issue in some areas. Concerns have been expressed that development pressures on Hilton Head, Daufuskie, and other prime barrier island development sites have served to substantially raise land values and to displace many of the minority families whose ancestors have lived in these areas since the 1800s.

There are a number of examples of state and local coastal agencies attempting to promote social diversity and inclusivity, typically through inclusionary housing programs and requirements. A significant example is the ambitious inclusionary housing program of the California Coastal Commission. Beginning in the late 1970s, the Commission attempted to promote inclusion through several means, including attempts to protect existing inexpensive units by denying condominium conversion proposals and requests to demolish low- and moderate-income housing. The Commission has also mandated the provision of a minimum number of affordable housing units in proposed condominium conversions and new housing projects (33% of units in condominiums of two units or more; 25% of units in new, nonrental residential projects of 15 units or more). Other states have mandated similar affordable housing provisions as part of their coastal programs (e.g., New Jersey's coastal program; Oregon requiring all localities to provide for a mixture of housing opportunities).

Urban Design and Protecting Community Character

Protecting the character and flavor of coastal communities is an important issue in many areas. Many coastal communities contain impressive historic buildings and resources that they wish to protect. A number of localities have sought to protect community character by instituting certain urban design review standards and processes. The coastal community of Canon Beach, Oregon, for instance, has outlawed the building of "formula food restaurants" (e.g., McDonalds, Pizza Huts). Other communities, such as Hilton Head, have mandated certain requirements for color, materials, and architectural style (they are proud that they now have a Red Roof Inn without a red roof). Increasingly, coastal communities are placing restrictions on billboards and signage, and imposing more stringent vegetation standards and requirements for visual buffers.

In new coastal developments there has been a renewed interest in incorporating those planning and design features that characterized early American towns and communities. These design features include grid streets, making public buildings and common spaces central, emphasizing pedestrian orientation, and the mixing of land uses (interspersing of commercial and residential uses), among others. Such a design philosophy has been referred to as "neo-traditionalism" and is strongly evident in such highly acclaimed coastal developments as Seaside on the Florida Gulf coast.

Conclusions

Coastal areas in the United States have been experiencing substantial growth in population and development in recent decades. Coastal counties are expected to have grown by some 60% between 1960 and 2010. With these development pressures come a host of environmental and land use conflicts and issues. Some of the more critical of these management issues have been identified and described here, and some clearly involve quite different notions of how the coastal zone ought to be used by the human species. The problems and challenges facing coastal managers are substantial. There is, however, an existing regulatory and management regime in place to address many of these issues, as well as substantial management activity at federal, state, regional, and local levels. The next several chapters attempt to briefly lay out the main contours of this framework, the types of coastal management programs and policies in place, and the extent to which they are successful or effective at accomplishing coastal management goals.

4

The Coastal
Management
Framework

A Fragmented Management Framework

Coastal management in the United States involves a number of key actors in both the public and the private sectors. In this chapter we briefly identify these key actors and the governmental agencies and jurisdictions which make up the current coastal management framework.

In the public sector, responsibility for coastal management in the United States is dispersed over a number of agencies at several jurisdictional levels. At the federal level, several different federal agencies have management responsibilities, including the National Oceanic and Atmospheric Administration (NOAA), especially the Office of Ocean and Coastal Resources Management (OCRM); the U.S. Environmental Protection Agency (USEPA); the U.S. Army Corps of Engineers (COE); the Federal Emergency Management Agency (FEMA); and several agencies with the Department of the Interior specifically, the National Park Service, the U.S. Fish and Wildlife Service, Minerals Management Service, and the Bureau of Land Management. These different agencies and the primary laws they are charged with implementing are listed in Table 4.1. While the OCRM (within NOAA) has primary responsibility for overseeing implementation of the federal Coastal Zone Management Act, each agency has important responsibilities and can influence in important ways activities that occur in the coastal zone. While the OCRM mission is exclusively

TABLE 4.1

Key Federal Agencies and Legislation Affecting the Coastal Zone

Agencies	Primary coastal management activities	Key authorizing legislation
Office of Ocean and Coastal Resource Management (OCRM within NOAA)	Implements coastal zone management program; works with states in developing and implementing their coastal zone programs	Coastal Zone Management Act (CZMA)
Federal Emergency Management Agency (FEMA)	Implements National Flood Insurance Program (NFIP); provides disaster assistance to coastal states and local governments	National Flood Insurance Act; Flood Disaster Protection Act; Stafford Disaster Relief and Emergency Assistance Act
U.S. Army Corps of Engineers (COE)	Technical assistance and funding of shoreline protection, beach renourishment; implements Section 404 wetlands permit program	Federal Flood Control Acts (of 1917, 1936, 1945, 1955, 1968 . . .); Clean Water Act
Environmental Protection Agency (EPA)	Oversees Section 404 wetlands permit program; establishes emission standards for air pollutants, effluent standards for water pollutants	Clean Water Act; Clean Air Act
National Park Service (NPS, within DOI)	Maintains and manages national seashores and national park system units; oversees Coastal Barrier Resources System (CBRS)	Coastal Barriers Resources Act (CoBRA)
U.S. Fish and Wildlife Service (USFWS, within DOI)	Enforces federal wildlife and endangered species laws; prepares and implements species recovery plans; establishes and maintains system of national wildlife refuges	Endangered Species Act (ESA)
National Marine Fisheries Service (NMFS within DOI)	Fisheries management; protection of marine mammals	Marine Mammal Protection Act

coastal zone management, its actual powers are limited, and it depends heavily on the initiative and management programs of state agencies.

No single agency at the federal level has control over coastal management, and there is currently no single or unified national coastal zone plan or strategy by which to guide or coordinate federal actions or programs. Although the Coastal Zone Management Act is an attempt at the federal level to establish national coastal management goals, objectives, and policies, it falls short of providing a framework for coordinating federal activities which may affect the coast. Coastal zone management responsibilities, then, are fragmented and dispersed at the federal level.

This fragmented system, moreover, has often resulted in situations where the programs and policies of different federal agencies work at cross-purposes. FEMA, for instance, has historically viewed its role as one of helping communities and states recover from disasters, and it provides extensive disaster relief following hurricanes and other coastal disaster events. While hazard mitigation has gained in importance in recent years, it can be argued that the provision of disaster relief and federally subsidized flood insurance, another key program administered by FEMA, serves to encourage hazardous development, working at cross-purposes to EPA, OCRM, and other agencies. The COE's focus on funding and constructing shoreline protection works (e.g., seawalls, jetties) and beach renourishment programs could also be perceived to work against the objectives of coastal resource protection. Responsibilities within a single program may also be shared. For instance, the Section 404 federal wetlands permitting program is jointly administered by the COE and USEPA (the COE issues permits in accordance with USEPA guidelines, and USEPA holds veto power over them). Important coastal management programs and authorities, then, are dispersed among a number of different federal agencies, and there does not currently exist a unified national strategy for managing the coastal zone. Proposals to consolidate these authorities have been made—for instance, out-going USEPA administrator William Reilly's proposal to fold NOAA into USEPA—but few improvements have yet been implemented in this regard.

In addition to a number of different federal agencies influencing the coastal zone, there are a number of specific pieces of federal legislation which have an impact on activities in the coastal zone, including the

Coastal Zone Management Act (CZMA), the National Flood Insurance Act, the Flood Disaster Protection Act, the Stafford Disaster Relief and Emergency Assistance Act, and the Coastal Barrier Resources Act (CoBRA), among others (see Table 4.1). Each of these programs is described in detail in Chapter 5.

The federal government has sought to shape and influence state and local management programs through the provision of financial and technical assistance (principally under CZMA) and to exercise (or impose) more direct regulatory controls over certain environmental resources within the coastal zone (e.g., wetlands, water quality). Federal legislation directly controls wetlands, water quality, air quality, and harbors and channels. In addition, the federal government has authority over all resources on federally owned land.

In addition to these explicit laws, programs, and policies influencing the coastal zone, there are other federal programs which represent *defacto* policy levers. The federal tax code, for example, can exercise a significant influence on coastal land use and development patterns. The code currently includes provisions which serve to subsidize hazardous development patterns. The casualty loss deduction, for instance, allows coastal property owners to deduct the cost of uninsured damages resulting from hurricanes and coastal storms. Other tax code subsidies include the interest and property tax deductions allowed for second homes and accelerated depreciation for seasonal rental properties. While these tax expenditures tend to be more "hidden," they nevertheless can serve to shape and influence development patterns and pressures.

A number of other federal programs and policies not specifically—or explicitly—coastal in nature can also exercise major influence. Federal funds for interstate highway construction have certainly served, in many cases, to open up coastal areas for major development pressures. Other federal activities which may influence coastal development include loan guarantees provided by the Farmers Home Administration, the Department of Housing and Urban Development, and the Department of Veterans Affairs. The Rural Electrification Administration and the U.S. Environmental Protection Agency have also played a role in providing infrastructure necessary for development.

Role of State and Local Governments

Much of the responsibility for actual control and management of coastal lands lies with coastal states and localities. The U.S. coastal management framework is clearly one of shared management between federal, state, and local jurisdictions. The federal government has played a major role in coastal management, and federal statutes and programs are often regarded as taking a lion's share of the regulatory power.

Effective and comprehensive coastal management, however, involves management and control of land use and growth, powers seen as legitimately reserved for state and local government. Historically, there has been substantial opposition toward, and suspicion of, federal efforts to impose land use controls or to otherwise circumvent state and local land use powers.

Each coastal state and territory exercises some degree of control over the coastal zone. Under CZMA, virtually all states, including oceanfront and Great Lakes states, have approved coastal management programs (29 out of 35 states, with Texas and Georgia each working toward developing a program) and are implementing certain management programs and policies. These programs include, for instance, directly regulating and controlling shorefront development (e.g., through an erosion-based setback standard such as imposed under North Carolina's Coastal Area Management Act) and development in other sensitive coastal lands (e.g., coastal marshes), acquisition of coastal lands and provision of beach access and recreational facilities, funding and undertaking beach reconstruction programs, and other provisions. States have played, and continue to play, an important role in coastal management, described in greater detail in Chapter 6.

Historically in the U.S. context, powers and responsibilities to manage land use and development have fallen heavily on local governments. Typically, coastal localities have authority (and indeed may be required) to adopt at least basic land use management tools, some of which include comprehensive and land use plans, zoning and subdivision ordinances, capital improvements programs, historic districts, exactions, land acquisition, taxation assessments, fees, and annexation.

Enactment of state coastal management programs often involves imposing new planning requirements on local governments. Under North Carolina's Coastal Area Management Act, coastal localities are required to prepare local comprehensive plans. These plans must satisfy certain minimum standards approved by the state (this program is described in greater detail in Chapter 6). Some coastal local governments have gone above and beyond these minimum state requirements, and several of the more progressive of these are described in later chapters.

Coastal ecosystems, or elements of the coastal ecosystem, often do not follow international, state, or local jurisdictional boundaries and, as a consequence, suggest the need for special regional substate or multistate governmental bodies. A coastal bay or estuary may encompass a large area and many different local jurisdictions (as in the case of San Francisco Bay) or several states (as in the case of the Chesapeake Bay). Examples of substate management and regulatory bodies include the San Francisco Bay Conservation and Development Commission (BCDC), the Puget Sound (Wash.) Regional Water Quality Management District, and the South Florida Regional Planning Council. There has been considerable interest at the federal level in promoting regional, ecosystem-based management efforts. These programs have included the National Estuary Program (NEP), under the federal Clean Water Act; the National Estuarine Reserve Research System (NERRS); and the preparation of Special Area Management Plans (SAMPs) under the CZMA.

Key Stakeholders in Coastal Management

Coastal policy and policy outcomes are clearly the result of political processes in which different factions and interest groups compete for attention and resources. Coastal management must be understood to occur within a political process, and actual coastal management decisions are very much the result of the interplay of these different stakeholder groups.

The stakeholders in coastal management policy are those major interest groups that seek to influence, or are influenced by, the allocation of coastal resources. Coastal policy in the United States is created by and for these stakeholders, who make up a network of public and private organizations.

This network creates our coastal policy and also serves as the framework for the implementation of resource management and water and land use regulation. Coastal policy in the United States is carried out by a unique blend of government and nongovernmental organizations, profit and nonprofit groups, and development and environmental advocates. Often policy coalitions compete with one another, each seeking to secure its own piece of the coastal resource pie. Despite the disparate viewpoints and multiplicity of agendas, a dynamic process continues to create a working system of policies, plans, and programs that affect the conservation and development of coastal areas and resources (Godschalk, 1992). The following paragraphs describe briefly some of the major stakeholders in coastal policy.

The first group of stakeholders is made up of the coastal states, the majority of which are officially part of the national coastal management program through the CZMA. The coastal states are represented by some of the more active state coastal program managers, such as California, Connecticut, Maryland, Massachusetts, Michigan, New Jersey, North Carolina, and Oregon. The Coastal States Organization (CSO), made up of gubernatorial delegates, also represents states' interests. The CSO was formed in 1970 to assure state representation in developing national coastal policy, and it continues to serve this purpose.

Coastal states are primarily interested in controlling coastal management initiatives within their jurisdiction by ensuring that any federal coastal policies remain flexible and allow individual states discretion over policy implementation. Many analysts believe the success of the national coastal management program is due in large part to its voluntary nature. National standards are set by NOAA in some areas, but whether and how the states choose to participate is left up to individual states.

Coastal states also have a strong interest in ensuring that the incentives for CZMA participation remain in place. One of these incentives is undoubtedly financial; the grants-in-aid programs have helped many states start up and continue innovative and effective programs for their coastal regions. The second major incentive is the consistency doctrine. By creating enforceable policy as a part of approved coastal programs, the states are assured that federal activities within the states' jurisdictions will not undermine state regulatory and management initiatives. Such a promise of federal consistency makes participation in the national coastal management system attractive to many states.

A second viable stakeholder in the coastal policy formation process includes coastal environmentalists, represented by a network of activist lawyers, national resource advocates, and academics (Godschalk, 1992). In some states, government agencies (for instance, departments of environmental protection and natural resources) often take a pro-active role in conservation issues. Some federal agencies, such as the U.S. Fish and Wildlife Service, also may take a resource protection and enhancement stance, and promote a tightening of the environmental and conservation aspects of coastal policy. Private organizations such as the Natural Resources Defense Council, the Sierra Club, The Nature Conservancy, and other environmental and public interest groups can also be influential in setting national priorities for coastal policy. These grassroots organizations can be a powerful force, and they are often quite visible and vocal in presenting their conservation agendas.

Coastal development interests make up another stakeholder group whose influence cannot be underestimated. This group is composed of powerful energy organizations such as the American Petroleum Institute, which calls for greater latitude in such areas as off-shore oil exploration and drilling. Development organizations such as the National Association of Homebuilders push for less regulation of private property to allow more development and greater density in coastal regions. These interest groups are often supported by local economic development advocates and chambers of commerce, which are anxious to see their communities grow to benefit the local citizenry and increase the tax base. Some government agencies also fall into this category, most notably the U.S. Army Corps of Engineers. While the Corps is given regulatory responsibility over certain coastal wetlands (Section 404 of the Federal Clean Water Act, administered by both the Corps and the EPA, contains permit provisions pertaining to the use and development of wetlands), it also plays a major role maintaining the navigability of the waters of the United States by dredging harbors, deepening channels, constructing bulkheads, and performing other tasks designed to allow commercial as well as recreational water transportation to take place. All these activities by this stakeholder group historically have focused on expanding coastal development opportunities (Godschalk, 1992).

Congress and congressional committees are important stakeholders since they are the writers of national coastal legislation, and they have historically played an integral role in the formulation of coastal policy. Particularly important congressional actors include the members and staffs of the House Merchant Marine and Fisheries Committee and the Senate Commerce Committee. The committees typically work to strengthen national coastal policy, but they also act as policy brokers, mediating the conflicting strategies of the different coastal coalitions (Godschalk, 1992).

The staff of the Office of Ocean and Coastal Resource Management are a final group of important stakeholders. This group includes both program-oriented career civil servants and their politically appointed chiefs (whose agendas may be at odds). Members of the staff play a vital role in implementation of the CZMA and work with the national interests in mind. OCRM is also responsive, however, to pressures from state, environmental, development, and congressional coalitions (Godschalk, 1992).

The stakeholders discussed above generally work within the framework provided by the National Coastal Management Program, accepting the core values embodied in the CZMA (Godschalk, 1992). The CZMA was set up originally to be collaborative in nature and fairly immune to one interest group or faction gaining complete control and dictating coastal policy for the nation.

Most of the stakeholders agree that managing growth so as to balance conservation and development in the coastal zone is a national priority, one that is best served by maintaining the voluntary, incentive-based intergovernmental program that has been created thus far. Most actors in the coastal policy process also believe that the states should be given discretionary power and considerable autonomy in defining their individual coastal programs to deal with their particular needs. National interests should also be a part of each state plan, with some universal standards applicable to all participants. Few stakeholders would also disagree with the operation of the consistency doctrine, requiring that federal activities within the coastal zone be consistent with approved state plans (Godschalk, 1992).

Despite consensus on some issues, the stakeholders do not agree on all the elements of the national coastal program. There has been persistent conflict between those interest groups that wish for increasing latitude and flexible standards, with freedom to develop and utilize coastal resources to the maximum extent feasible, and those that argue for more stringent regulation of the natural environment and for the requirement of more explicit standards in all state plans (Godschalk, 1992). The result is a constant process of balancing and juggling between flexibility and rigor, development and conservation, regulation and laissez-faire.

When discussing stakeholders, it is crucial to consider those groups and individuals that do not reach the forefront of policy-making and yet who have a definite "stake" in the coastal region. Many whose very livelihood depends on the viability of coastal ecosystems may not be recognized as stakeholders and therefore not be invited to the discussion table when coastal policy is being formulated. Local populations along the coast may all too frequently fall into this category of unrecognized stakeholder. The fisherman who depends on healthy waters to support his catch; the clamdigger who relies on mudflats left untainted by upriver pollution; the beachfront cottage owner who comes seasonally for rest, relaxation, and a beautiful view—all these individuals have come to depend on the coast as a way of life, and yet too often such people are not involved in the high-stakes discussions which affect their futures.

Finally, we must include in our discussion of stakeholders the elected official. Certainly at the local level, and at the state and federal levels as well, representatives of the people must champion the cause of coastal management, both in terms of economic health for local communities and preservation of the ecosystem. Through their representatives in government, residents, workers, visitors, and others with an interest in the coastal regions of our nation can have their voices be heard in the formation of coastal policy.

Conclusions

This chapter has provided a broad overview of the coastal management framework in the United States. Coastal management occurs in a fragmented framework, with responsibilities and authorities shared by federal, state, and local governmental bodies. At the federal level, agencies such as the Office of Ocean and Coastal Resources Management, the U.S. Army Corps of Engineers, Federal Emergency Management Agency, and the U.S. Environmental Protection Agency are major actors. Much of the actual "on the ground" management in the U.S. framework, however, occurs at state and local levels. Local governments have historically had the primary responsibility for land use planning and community land use decisions, although increasingly states have exercised direct control over development and other activities occurring in the coastal zone.

Coastal zone management is very much a political process and involves a number of key actors and interest groups in addition to government agencies. These different coastal stakeholders, groups have different perspectives on coastal management, and coastal management decisions are often the result of the interplay of these different groups.

5

Federal Coastal Policy

The Federal Role in Coastal Zone Management

As Chapter 4 suggested, the federal government plays an increasingly important role in coastal management. One of the major ways the federal government has traditionally controlled land use activities in the coastal zone as elsewhere is through real-property ownership. The federal government, through several different agencies and departments, is by far the single largest land holder in the United States. The National Park Service, the U.S. Fish and Wildlife Service of the Department of the Interior, the National Forest Service in the Department of Agriculture, and the Bureau of Land Management own vast acreage throughout the country. Military installations and outer continental shelf property also represent significant holdings of the federal government. While the greatest share of this federally controlled land is located inland, a sizable portion is along our coastline.

The federal government also served an early role in coastal management by means of the Commerce Clause of the U.S. Constitution, which grants Congress the power to "regulate commerce with foreign nations and among the several states" (Art. I, Sec. 8, Cl. 3). Supreme Court decisions have maintained that the authority to regulate commerce extends the authority to regulate navigation, including control over navigable waters. This right of the federal government is called the navigation servitude. The navigation servitude is the right to compel the removal of any obstruction to navigation. This right is paramount, and therefore there is no necessity to pay just compensation ordinarily required by the Fifth Amendment for a taking of private property.

The U.S. Army Corps of Engineers has been delegated the power to carry out the mandate of the Commerce Clause and to maintain the navigability of the waters of the United States. To perform this function, the Corps has engaged in a vast array of civil works projects for decades, including dredging channels, building breakwaters, and constructing harbor facilities. The Corps also regulates other participants' activities in the coastal zone primarily through issuance and enforcement of permits.

One of the earliest federal permit statutes is the Rivers and Harbors Act of 1899. Section 10 of the Act forbids excavation or construction in "navigable waters" without approval of the Secretary of the Army. There has been dispute over the exact jurisdiction of the Corps in terms of navigable waters, but activities occurring outside of, but which affect, navigable waters may in some cases also be covered by Section 10.

The federal role expanded exponentially in the early 1970s with the passage of the federal Coastal Zone Management Act (CZMA). The passage of this Act acknowledged simultaneously the fact that our coastlines represent resources of tremendous national value, and that the existing programs at state and local levels were inadequate to protect them or ensure their wise use.

While the CZMA represents a milestone for federal involvement in managing the coastal zone, the program it created is but one piece of the federal puzzle. In this chapter we review in some detail the major components of federal coastal policy, in addition to the CZMA. Chapter 6 details some of the programs and activities undertaken by the states largely as a result of the Act.

Coastal Zone Management Act

In many ways the CZMA does represent the cornerstone of federal efforts at promoting the protection and management of our nation's coastlines. Enacted in 1972, the Act grew out of growing public concern for the environment, including ocean and coastal ecosystems and resources. The federal Stratton Commission's 1969 report, *Our Nation and the Sea*, was instrumental in focusing the attention of citizens, politicians, and scientists toward the importance of coastal regions and the lack of effective management. Several coastal management bills were introduced in Congress following issuance of the Stratton Report;

most of the legislation emphasized *either* development *or* conservation. The Act which finally was passed in 1972 provided a unique combination of goals—the National Oceanic and Atmospheric Administration (NOAA) would administer a voluntary, federal grant-in-aid program which would encourage individual coastal states to promote a balance between development and the environment through coastal land use planning and management.

A Collaborative Strategy

The CZMA represents a unique federal–state collaboration. Specifically, the Act sought to provide incentives for coastal states to prepare and implement management plans, largely through the provision of financial and technical assistance. Under Section 305 of the CZMA, federal monies are made available to states for the preparation of management plans; and under Section 306, funds are available for the implementation of these plans once approved. Monies are provided on a cost-share basis. Initial grants provided by Section 305 have covered up to two-thirds of the costs of program development. Section 306 grants have also covered up to two-thirds of the costs of administering a state's coastal management program. Presently, however, the cost-share is 50-50 federal/state. As Table 5.1 indicates, some $70,000 in Section 305 program development and $341,000 in Section 306 program administration monies have been provided to states.

A second major incentive for state participation is provided through Section 307 of the Act, which requires all future projects and actions to be "consistent," to the maximum extent practicable, with state management plans. Specifically, Section 307(c)(1)(A) states that "each federal agency activity within or outside the coastal zone that affects any land or water use or natural resource of the coastal zone shall be carried out in a manner which is consistent to the maximum extent practicable with the enforceable policies of approved state management programs." Federal actions covered by the consistency requirements include navigational and flood control projects, Section 404 wetlands permits, highway development, airport plans, wastewater treatment plant funding, military activities, and fisheries management. Through federal consistency, many states saw the opportunity to gain some measure of control over federal actions and policies in the coastal zone.

The consistency provisions of the CZMA have had mixed results.

TABLE 5.1

Coastal Program Expenditures, Fiscal Years 1974–1988

Section		Amount ($)	Percentage of total
305	Program development	69,720	10.02
306	Program administration (implementation)	341,477	49.08
308	CEIP	239,217	34.38
309	Interstate coordination	4,208	00.60
310	Research and technical assistance	236	00.03
315.1	Estuarine reserves	33,589	04.83
P.L. 92-532	(Marine sanctuaries)	6,733	00.97
TOTAL (does not add due to rounding)		$695,775	

Implementation of the doctrine has been generally successful. The body of consistency decisions by the Secretary of Commerce appears to strike a balance between state interests and coastal programs and national economic and security interests. Based on this record, it is clear that federal development projects in the coastal zone, as well as private development projects that require a federal permit, are subject to state coastal management policies and may be substantially modified at the insistence of the states to conform to these policies.

However, there have been several highly publicized controversies over consistency between coastal managers and conservationists on the one hand and federal officials and industry on the other. These disputes have generally involved offshore oil and gas exploration and development, dredge-spoil disposal, and incineration activities. Furthermore, confusion and disagreement over the application of the consistency doctrine continue to arise. The 1990 amendments to the CZMA have attempted to clarify the legal status of federal consistency and its role in coastal management.

The CZMA specifies certain things that must be in state coastal management plans. Specifically, plans must include the following:

- identification of boundaries of the coastal zone

- definition of permissible land and water uses within the coastal zone

- inventory and designation of areas of particular concern
- identification of means by which states propose to exert control over land and water uses, including list of relevant constitutional provisions, legislative enactments, regulations, etc.
- broad guidelines on priority uses in particular areas, including specifically those uses of lowest priority
- description of organizational structure proposed to implement the management program, including responsibilities and interrelationships of local, areawide, state, regional, and interstate agencies in the management process

State plans must be reviewed and approved by the Office of Ocean and Coastal Resources Management (OCRM). The Secretary of Commerce has the authority to withdraw funding if the coastal state fails to adhere to "the terms of any grant or cooperative agreement" (16 C.F.R. §1458(c)(1)(B)). If the coastal state fails to take the proper steps upon being notified of suspension of financial assistance, the Secretary is authorized to withdraw approval of the state's management plan (16 C.F.R. §1458(d)).

An Evolving Law

The CZMA has been amended and reauthorized nine times since its enactment in 1972. The program, as a consequence, has evolved and changed over that time. The 1976 amendments enacted the Coastal Energy Impact Program (CEIP), largely in response to the ensuing energy crisis. The CEIP was to advance the nation's self-sufficiency for energy by providing federal funds to meet states' needs resulting from new or expanded energy activities in the coastal zone. During the Reagan Administration, Congress continued to fund and reauthorize the CZMA, despite the President's repeated attempts to zero-budget the CZMA appropriations and to phase out federal CZMA and CEIP programs. By the early 1980s, individual state programs were being implemented and the coastal states were supportive of Congressional efforts to continue the CZMA.

In 1980 the Coastal Zone Management Improvement Act was enacted to guide the states' implementation process, and it introduced a new national policy defining the following nine areas of national interest which the states must address: natural resource protection, hazards management, major facility siting, public access, urban waterfront and port redevelopment, simplification of decision procedures, intergovernmental coordination, public participation, and living marine resource conservation. In 1986, the 99th Congress passed the Coastal Zone Management Reauthorization Act, which continued the program, but reduced its spending.

At the end of the 1980s, Congress again reassessed the goals, priorities, and procedures of the federal coastal program. The Bush Administration appropriated funds to continue state implementation of the CZMA. The 1990 amendments to the CZMA reaffirmed and enhanced the federal program as a comprehensive and innovative management bill. Several new initiatives were introduced, including a major new coastal nonpoint source pollution program (Section 6217) and an enhancement grants program. These two programs are described briefly below.

Under Section 6217 an ambitious new program to address nonpoint source pollutants was mandated. Specifically, 6217 requires states to prepare a Coastal Nonpoint Pollution Control Program. States must adopt management measures in conformity with the guidance document published by EPA and NOAA. To receive approval from both agencies, the states must, at a minimum, include the following six elements in their nonpoint program:

- a description of a range of methods, measures, or practices designed to control nonpoint source pollutants

- a description of the categories and subcategories of activities and locations for which each measure may be suitable

- an identification of the individual pollutants or categories or classes of pollutants which may be controlled by the measures and the water quality effect of the measures

- quantitative estimates of the pollution reduction effects and costs of the measures

- a description of the factors which should be taken into account in adopting the measures to specific sites or locations

- necessary monitoring techniques to accompany the measures to assess over time their success in reducing pollution loads and improving water quality

Sanctions are levied on states that fail to submit a program which meets the requirements of Section 6217. Sanctions include a reduction of federal grant monies for both nonpoint source and coastal zone management programs.

The 1990 reauthorization also created a new Coastal Zone Enhancement Grants Program, which reflects and identifies certain management areas deemed by Congress to represent priorities. Under the program, states are encouraged to address eight specific issues:

- protection of coastal wetlands or creation of new coastal wetlands

- mitigation of natural hazards (including potential sea level rise and Great Lakes level rise)

- increasing opportunities for public access

- reducing marine debris

- addressing cumulative and secondary impacts of coastal growth

- preparing and implementing special area management plans

- planning for ocean resources

- procedures and policies for siting energy facilities

Other Key Federal Programs Influencing Coastal Development

What follows below is a brief description and discussion of several of the other key federal programs, policies, and laws which influence coastal growth and development and further comprise the federal government's *defacto* coastal management policies. Specifically, the following programs are considered: the National Flood Insurance Program, federal disaster assistance, shoreline protection and beach renourishment, Coastal Barrier Resources Act, the Clean Water Act (including Section 404 and the National Estuary Program), the National Estuary Reserve Research System, and the National Marine Sanctuaries Program.

National Flood Insurance Program

The availability of federal flood insurance is frequently cited as a primary example of how hazardous coastal development is subsidized and how the wrong kind of incentives are created. Federal flood insurance was made available in 1968 through the enactment of the National Flood Insurance Act. Prior to this program affordable private flood insurance was generally not available. (A similar reluctance of private insurers to provide wind insurance has led to the establishment of wind pools in states such as Florida and Texas.) Under the National Flood Insurance Program (NFIP), federally subsidized flood insurance is made available to owners of flood-prone property in participating communities. Coverage is available both for the structure itself (up to $185,000 for a single family structure) and for contents (up to $60,000). Administered by FEMA—Federal Insurance Administration (FIA), in particular—participating communities are required to adopt certain minimum floodplain management standards, including restrictions on new development in designated floodways (development within the floodway is prohibited if it results in raising flood levels more than one foot), a requirement that new structures in the 100-year flood zone be elevated to at or above the 100-year flood level (generally known as base flood elevation, or BFE), and a requirement that subdivisions are designed to minimize exposure to flood hazards. For high-hazard coastal zones ("velocity" zones, or "V" zones), additional standards are imposed, including the requirement that buildings must be elevated on pilings, all new development must be landward of mean high water, that the BFE includes potential wave heights, and that new development must not damage dunes or dune vegetation.

While program participation is entirely voluntary, strong incentives currently exist in the program. Because of limited participation in the early years of the program, the 1973 Flood Disaster Protection Act mandated flood insurance for all federally backed mortgages (e.g., VA, FHA) and mortgages and loans obtained through federally insured and regulated financial institutions. Also, disaster assistance grants (public assistance) are not available to local governments not participating in the program (individual property owners need not have flood insurance to be eligible for individual and family grants, however). As a result, community participation has been high, with about 19,000 localities participating. While participation rates for owners of flood-prone property have been fairly low (about 25% of those eligible), this nevertheless amounts to a considerable federal financial liability. There are currently approximately 2.5 million flood policies in effect, representing nearly $230 billion in insurance liability (FEMA, 1992). The NFIP is the second largest financial obligation at the federal level (social security being the largest). It is estimated that more than 70% of the NFIP policyholders are located in coastal communities, with many of these located in the most hazardous locations (some 64,000 in V zones; see Miller 1989).

Damage claims under NFIP have been substantial over the years. Since 1978 there have been 350,000 claims, with total payments of more than $2.5 billion (FEMA, 1992). (These figures do not include claims arising from Hurricanes Andrew and Iniki.) A relatively high percentage of these damage losses have occurred in coastal communities. For communities which contain velocity zones there have been some 240,000 claims over this same period, paying out nearly $1.7 billion. Thus, approximately 68% of the claims since 1978 have been in coastal communities, and 68% of the funds paid out have been for damages there (FEMA, 1992).

Historically, the NFIP has suffered from a number of problems and has been the subject of considerable criticism. A major point of contention between supporters and detractors of the program is whether it is in fact actuarially sound and thus pays for itself. In the last several years, beginning with fiscal year 1987, the NFIP has in fact been generating a surplus (i.e., premiums payments have exceeded claims). As of September 1992 the flood insurance fund contained about $416 million (FEMA, 1992a). However, the program has generated deficits over much of its lifetime. Between 1978 and 1987 the program ran an average annual operating deficit of about $65 million, generating a $657 million deficit over that 10-year period (Miller, 1989). Between 1969 and 1986 the program was supported by Congressional appropriations of $1.2 billion and about $2.5 billion from policyholders. Even in recent years, while the program has been financially self-sufficient, operating deficits have occurred. (In fiscal years 1989 and 1992 total program expenses have exceeded total income.)

There is little dispute that the extent of the surplus in the flood insurance fund in recent months has been quite modest when compared to potential flood damage liabilities. Even FIA's own estimates suggest

TABLE 5.2

Estimated Probabilities of Exceeding
Given Levels of Flood Insurance Losses

Total annual loss ($ millions)	Estimated exceedence probability (%)
300	60–70
800	30–35
1,400	10–15
1,800	2–7
3,500	0.05–0.5

Source: FEMA (1992).

that the probability is quite great of exceeding in any given year the existing surplus amounts. As Table 5.2 indicates (generated by FEMA), the probability of total annual losses of $800 million or greater is a high 30–35% and an even higher 60–70% probability of exceeding $300 million (FEMA 1992b) (The FEMA director can borrow up to $500 million from the Treasury without notifying Congress and an additional $500 million if Congress is notified.) FEMA has estimated that its probable maximum loss in any given year is as high as $3.5 billion, much greater even than its present $1 billion borrowing authority (FEMA, 1992b). Some have argued that FEMA's ability even to borrow funds in this amount from the federal treasury without Congressional approval has reduced necessary oversight of the program. It is also important again to remember that the nation has experienced over the last 30 years an abnormally low level of hurricane and coastal storm activity.

In comparison to the magnitude of potential liabilities under the program and the meager size of the current surplus (and, in effect, a cause) is the modest cost of these insurance benefits to property owners. The average cost of flood insurance is by all measures quite low. According to the General Accounting Office (GAO), the average annual cost is $262 for all structures and $469 for structures in coastal high-hazard zones.

Other significant problems in the implementation of the NFIP have also been identified. While flood insurance is virtually mandatory for new construction (requiring mortgages from federally insured banks), there is considerable evidence that many lenders are not ensuring that the requirement is satisfied. It has been estimated that there are approximately 11 million properties in Special Flood Hazard Areas (SFHAs 100—year floodplain), but only about 1.4 million are actually covered by flood insurance policies. A 1990 GAO study of compliance in two states, Maine and Texas, found relatively high levels of non-compliance (22% and 78%, respectively, of properties in SFHAs in Maine and Texas requesting disaster assistance did not have insurance). Interviews with lending institutions uncovered a variety of problems, including erroneous classification of properties and allowing insurance policies to lapse later on (see GAO, 1990). This study illustrated as well that many properties in flood hazard areas simply are not required by law to have flood insurance, either because they have no mortgage or have a mortgage from an unregulated lender (essentially institutions not federally insured). Also, enforcement and monitoring staff within FEMA are sparse, and ensuing full compliance with mandated floodplain management requirements remains a concern.

A general criticism of NFIP is that it is not run as a private insurance company would be, with loss reduction always in mind. A relatively high percentage of all flood insurance claims—about 43% (according to the GAO)—have been for repetitively damaged properties. Yet in these cases, FEMA does not, as perhaps a private insurance company would, cut off or substantially restrict future coverage for such properties. Individuals are permitted to rebuild and to continue to receive insurance, and the program allows for a potentially unlimited process of damage-rebuild-damage. Many believe that the premiums charged to repetitive loss properties should at least be raised by FEMA in these instances to reflect the actual occurrence and recurrence of flood events.

Another significant concern about NFIP as it functions in coastal areas is its failure to take into account long-term erosion. In fact, Congress initiated changes in 1973 to the definition of "flood" to include collapse or subsidence along shorelines, and NFIP regulations were amended to allow creation of special erosion zones ("areas of special flood-related erosion hazards" or "Zone E") and to mandate local land management programs to take these hazards into account (see NRC, 1990). However, no special erosion zones have even been delineated, and FEMA has not sought to require local land management programs (i.e., setbacks) to address erosion hazards. Moreover, long-term erosion trends are generally not taken into account in current FEMA floodplain mapping. The V zones, or velocity zones, are the closest flood zone to a shoreline erosion zone, yet they are often narrowly drawn and "frequently exclude adjoining areas with virtually indistinguishable hazard characteristics" (NRC, 1990, p. 75).

Another problem is the infrequency with which flood insurance maps are revised and updated. It has been estimated that FEMA is able to remap communities on average every nine years. Yet, many participating communities are rapidly growing, and substantial development and building in the floodplain can substantially modify local flood hazards.

For new construction occurring in flood hazard zones, the NFIP clearly has led the effort, however, of imposing stronger building standards, notably through elevation requirements. Newer, elevated structures on pilings have clearly performed better in recent coastal storm events, and in this sense the NFIP has had a positive effect. Under NFIP these new construction standards are also imposed during reconstruction under its "substantial improvement" provisions. Until recently this has had the positive effect of requiring structures damaged 50% or greater to conform to the newer FEMA elevation and construction standards, resulting in the replacement of older, vulnerable structures with safer elevation structures. Recently, however, FEMA has changed these requirements (largely in response to the danger from Hurricane Andrew) so that local floodplain ordinances now can interpret this 50% rule in terms of "replacement value," such that if the damage done to a structure does not exceed 50% of the cost to replace the building then it need not adhere to the new construction standards. Thus, through this new standard FEMA is essentially allowing heavily damaged structures to be rebuilt without having to satisfy newer, more stringent elevation and construction standards that could at least make coastal development patterns somewhat safer.

An Evolving Flood Insurance Program: Section 1362, Upton–Jones and Community Rating System

The NFIP, despite the limitations cited here, has evolved gradually over the years, and certain programs and provisions have been developed which move it in the direction of greater hazard mitigation and loss reduction. One of the more significant of these is the Section 1362

Flooded Properties Purchase Program. Authorized by a section of the Flood Insurance Act, the program allows FEMA to break the damage-rebuild-damage cycle, which accounts for many damage claims.

Under the program, FEMA offers to buy out owners of damaged property, paying the difference between the fair market value of the structure and the allowable insurance claim, plus the value of the land on which the structure is/was located. The community, however, must agree to participate, must be willing to accept the land, and must prepare a plan for its use which ensures that it will never be developed in the future. Eligible properties must have had federal flood insurance and must meet one of several damage criteria (e.g., damaged substantially beyond repair or damaged at least 25% three times in last five years).

While the 1362 program makes a great deal of sense, it has been used sparingly. Modest amounts of funds are set aside for 1362 purchases. Since first funded in 1980, FEMA has acquired only about 100 properties per year, and there has been a clear bias against using 1362 funds in coastal areas. The feeling is that because of the often very high cost of land in coastal communities, it is possible to get a greater "bang for the buck" when these limited funds are employed in riverine locations. Since 1980, Congress has appropriated less than $5 million per year for 1362, and in some cases FEMA has failed even to use all of these monies. Several recent Congressional bills intended to reform the NFIP extend and expand the 1362 concept.

One of the largest examples of the use of Section 1362 monies in a coastal area involved a 300-home subdivision in Baytown, Texas, devastated by Hurricane Alicia (1983). Located along the Galveston Bay, the Brownwood Subdivision had been repeatedly flooded in the past and had become increasingly vulnerable through gradual subsidence (a consequence of oil and water extraction in the Galveston/Houston area). Following Alicia, the city of Baytown imposed a moratorium on rebuilding, and FEMA made 1362 monies available to eligible property owners willing to sell out. Through the 1362 program, rebuilding in this extremely dangerous area was effectively prevented, the land retained in open space, and a potentially endless string of flood insurance claims ended. (For a discussion of the Baytown case, see Godschalk et al., 1989.)

Another major improvement in the flood insurance program was passage of the so-called Upton–Jones Amendment to the Housing and Community Development Act of 1987, which sought to make available funds to subsidize demolition or relocation of those shoreline structures subject to fairly immediate erosion hazards. The amendment was co-sponsored by Representatives Fred Upton (R-Michigan) and Walter Jones (D-North Carolina) and was a direct result of the erosion hazards existing in both of their states. Upton, concerned with the public safety and debris problems created by shoreline structures damaged and destroyed as a result of rising lake levels along the Great Lakes, sought to make funds available for demolition. Jones was responding to the high number of structures in North Carolina vulnerable to short-term erosion; it was estimated that 750 oceanfront structures, and some 5,000 structures located within the 60-year erosion line, would be lost to erosion in the next 10 years in North Carolina (see NRC, 1990).

Under the NFIP prior to Upton–Jones, a property owner could not receive any flood insurance payment until the structure was actually damaged. Under Upton–Jones, owners of shorefront property with federal flood insurance are eligible for sizable demolition or relocation subsidies. Specifically, Upton–Jones provides up to 40% of the insured value of a building for relocation (or 40% of the cost of relocation if less) and up to 100% of the insured value of a structure for demolition plus 10% (or the cost of demolition if less than 10%). Relocation funds can be used for, among other things, new site preparation, construction of a new foundation, utility hookups, etc.

For structures to qualify they must be certified to be within a zone of imminent collapse. FEMA defines this area as seaward of a line 10 feet plus five times the average annual rate of erosion (see Figure 5.1). The provisions also require the state or local government to condemn structures, or certify that they are in danger of collapse, in order for them to qualify. Once FEMA declares a structure subject to imminent collapse, the property owner has a certain reasonable time to relocate or demolish, after which he or she is only entitled to 40% of covered losses in the next storm or flooding event.

Once demolition or relocation occurs, certain restrictions are placed on the availability of new insurance. Specifically, any future development on the property must, in order to receive flood insurance, locate landward of the 30-year erosion line (for structures of 1 to 4 dwelling

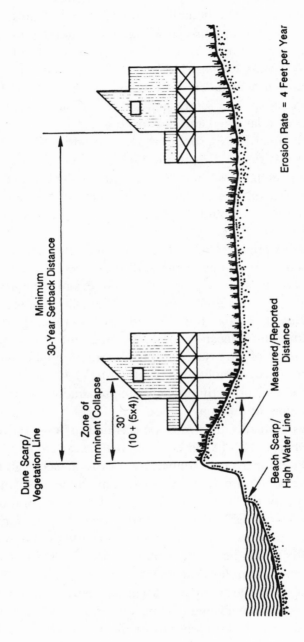

Figure 5.1 Example of determination of zone of imminent collapse and 30-year setback distance. (From NRC, 1990.)

units) or landward of the 60-year line in the case of larger structures. Structures moved to a different site must also meet these standards, as well as the elevation and other floodplain management restrictions which exist there.

To date, use of Upton–Jones has been limited. As of August 1989, only 266 claims had been filed. According to a recent National Research Council study, there are a number of reasons which help to explain low participation, including a general lack of awareness about the program, a reluctance to remove or interrupt income from rental properties, a lack of suitable or affordable relocation sites, a lack of eligibility for land acquisition, and problems encountered in condemnation of structures (many states do not allow condemnation unless there is actual structural damage, a situation that will require changes to state law to rectify).

While there has been much support for Upton–Jones in concept, recommendations for improvement of the program have been made. The National Research Council report recommends the following changes: (1) encourage relocation over demolition, (2) mandate relocation behind the 30-year erosion line, (3) require an easement or some other form of legal restriction preventing use of vacated shorefront areas, and (4) terminate insurance or raise insurance premiums for those structures certified as within the zone of imminent collapse, if they are not relocated or demolished after a certain time. Some have also criticized the program for defining the eligible zone of imminent collapse too narrowly, suggesting that structures landward of the five-year erosion line should also be encouraged to relocate. The program could also be criticized as providing yet an additional underwriting by the public of private risks (i.e., will it further encourage risky coastal development if property owners know they will be able to receive such relocation assistance in the future?). The suggested changes mentioned above, in addition to coupling program benefits to more stringent erosion management for new construction (e.g., coastal setbacks) would serve to substantially eliminate such incentives.

In recent years FEMA has also initiated a new program called the community rating system (CRS), which seeks to reward communities for the additional activities and programs they undertake, beyond the minimum requirements of NFIP, which serve to minimize flood damages. Specifically, the insurance premiums of property owners within these communities are reduced to take into account these local activities. Participation in CRS is voluntary, and local governments are responsible for submitting the documentation which shows implementation of these different creditable activities.

There are 18 mitigation activities for which CRS gives credit, grouped in four categories (see Table 5.3). These four categories include public information, mapping and regulations, flood damage reduction, and flood preparedness. Communities are assigned a certain number of points for these activities, depending on the extent and

TABLE 5.3

Eighteen Mitigation Activities in the CRS Program

Activity	Maximum points	Average points	Applicants (%)
300 Public information activities			
310 Elevation certificates	137[a]	73	100
320 Map determinations	140	140	92
330 Outreach projects	175	59	53
340 Hazard disclosure	81[a]	39	40
350 Flood protection library	25	20	77
360 Flood protection assistance	66	51	45
400 Mapping and regulatory activities			
410 Additional flood data	360[a]	60	20
420 Open space preservation	450[a]	115[b]	42
430 Higher regulatory standards	785[a]	101[a]	59
440 Flood data maintenance	120[a]	41	41
450 Stormwater management	380[a]	121	37
500 Flood damage reduction activities			
510 Repetitive loss projects	441[a]	41	11
520 Acquisition and relocation	1,600	97	13
530 Retrofitting	1,400	23	3
540 Drainage system maintenance	330[a]	226	82
600 Flood preparedness activities			
610 Flood warning program	200[a]	173	5
620 Levee safety	900[a]	0	0
630 Dam safety	120[a]	64	45

Source: FEMA (1992e).

[a]Maximum points revised since 1990 *CRS Schedule*.

[b]1990 credits revised to reflect 1992 *CRS Schedule*.

likely effectiveness at achieving CRS objectives. A maximum number of credits is established for each measure, and a detailed coordinators manual lays out the methodology for assigning points for the various measures. The CRS program calls for periodic review and monitoring, and adjustments to assigned points.

For each particular measure a detailed point allocation methodology has been developed (see FEMA, 1992e). The points generated from each individual measure are then added up to produce the community's total points, which are then used to determine the extent of premium reduction for property owners. As Table 5.4 indicates, premium reductions range from 5% to 45% for property within SFHAs (i.e., A and V zones). A maximum 5% reduction is allowed for property outside of SFHAs, largely on the grounds that premiums are already low in these areas and because the measures for which credits are given are directed at the 100-year flood zones.

Participation in the CRS program has so far been modest in terms of the number of communities. For fiscal year 1992 there were 564 communities (or only about 3% of the 19,000 communities participating in the NFIP). However, despite this small percentage, this does represent about 45% of the flood insurance policy base. The level of mitigation effort for most participating communities has been

TABLE 5.4

Premium Reductions Based on the
Eighteen Mitigation Factors

Community's total points	Class	SFHA credit (%)	Non-SFHA credit (%)
4,500+	1	45	5
4,000–4,499	2	40	5
3,500–3,999	3	35	5
3,000–3,499	4	30	5
2,500–2,999	5	25	5
2,000–2,499	6	20	5
1,500–1,999	7	15	5
1,000–1,499	8	10	5
500–999	9	5	5
0–499	10	0	0

Source: FEMA (1992e).

relatively low, with the vast majority of these communities—519 (or about 92%)—certified as class 9 communities, or undertaking sufficient mitigation measures to present a 5% reduction in policyholder premiums. Another 40 communities have been certified as class 8 (10% reductions), four communities as class 7 (15% reduction), and one community as class 5 (25% reduction) (FEMA, 1993).

Questions nevertheless remain about the CRS strategy. It is not clear that the most active local governments would not be undertaking these kinds of mitigation actions anyway. It is also not clear that some of the measures for which local governments are given credit, such as hazard disclosure, do in fact lead to clear hazard or damage reduction. Moreover, such an approach could be criticized for further reducing the premiums paid and in fact further subsidizing hazardous development patterns. As an alternative, a number of the measures for which localities are given (e.g., an erosion setback) could simply be made mandatory as conditions of participation in NFIP.

Federal Disaster Assistance

The federal government has for many years been involved in assisting state and local governments in responding to, and recovering from, national disasters. Such financial assistance can be seen as another form of incentive for hazardous coastal development by subsidizing the riskiness of public and private actions. The federal disaster assistance framework was substantially revamped in 1988, when Congress passed the Robert T. Stafford Disaster Relief and Emergency Assistance Act, which provides greater emphasis and financial support for mitigation activities (see below).

Several major forms of disaster assistance are available through FEMA. Such assistance generally falls into two categories: (1) individual and family assistance and (2) public assistance.

Under FEMA's Individual and Family Grants (IFG) program, grants of aid up to $10,040 can be made to individuals and families to cover disaster-related expenses (e.g., home repairs not covered through insurance, replacement of personal belongings). Under FEMA's public assistance program, states and communities can receive grants, usually at a 75%/25% federal cost share, to cover the cost of damages to public facilities. Eligible projects include repair and replacement of roads, bridges, sewer and water systems, recreational facilities, and replacement of artificial public beaches, etc. Communities not participating in the National Flood Insurance Program are not eligible for public assistance funds. Applicants under the IFG program need not be in a participating community, nor have purchased federal flood insurance (though they must agree to purchase it as a condition of receiving such grants).

Precisely how much of an impact federal disaster assistance has, or has had, in encouraging (or failing to discourage) hazardous and damaging coastal development is uncertain. Amounts of federal disaster assistance in recent years have been substantial. Some $8.3 billion was spent between 1978 and 1988 on presidentially declared disasters. FEMA reports that approximately $885 million (or about $88.5 million per year) was spent as a result of hurricanes and coastal storm events (Miller, 1989). These FEMA disaster assistance monies do provide a significant subsidy for coastal communities, underwriting risk to a variety of coastal public investments. Public assistance monies are generally provided on a 75/25 cost share (75% federal/25% state or local) and can be used to repair and restore such public investments as roads, sewer and water systems, public boardwalks, and even loss of beach renourishment sand. In several recent disasters, including Hurricanes Andrew and Hugo, the federal government agreed to cover 100% of the costs of these public-sector damages. Where the 25% contribution has been required, frequently the state assumes half, leaving local governments to assume only 12.5% of the cost of such damages.

There are currently no provisions in this system to consider the magnitude of the damage to an individual community or to consider the financial capability of the state or locality to cover these damages. What results is an incentive system in which high-risk communities have little incentive to ensure that public facilities are placed in safe locations or designed in ways that minimize future vulnerability to hurricanes or other disasters. And in may cases the federal reconstruction subsidy is in addition to the original federal subsidy used to construct the facility or investment. For example, the federal government heavily subsidizes beach renourishment (through the U.S. Army Corps of Engineers; see below), and once sand is lost or heavily eroded in a storm event, this becomes an eligible cost under the public assistance program.

Disaster assistance has in may ways been seen by states and

communities as an entitlement and something deserved regardless of the extent or cause of the damages or of the ability of these jurisdictions to assume these costs. In theory, presidential disaster declarations are only to be issued where the resources of affected states and local governments are clearly exceeded. Yet, presidential declarations have been increasingly viewed as pro forma and have occurred even where damage levels are relatively modest and where state and local governments could clearly have assumed the cost with little burden.

In its defense FEMA has sought to reform this system in the past only to be harshly critized by state and local government representatives and owners of property in high-risk areas. Proposals were made, for example, in the mid-1980s to increase the required state–local share of public assistance grants to 50/50 (i.e., 50% federal, 50% state/local) and to impose a set of ability-to-pay criteria. These proposals received considerable political flack and were eventually dropped. Many commentators, however, have echoed the need for such reforms, which might, among others, help to reduce this negative incentive structure (e.g., Burby, 1990).

In addition to FEMA, a number of other federal agencies provide some form of disaster assistance. These include loans, grants, and reconstruction monies from the Small Business Administration, the Federal Highway Administration (for roads and bridges), the Department of Education (for school buildings), the Farmers Home Administration, the U.S. Army Corps of Engineers, and the Economic Development Administration, among others.

There have also been some positive changes to the federal disaster assistance framework in recent years. The Stafford Act created a Hazard Mitigation Grants Program (HMGP, Section 404), for instance, which provides federal matching funds for state and local mitigation projects (i.e., the federal government will pick up 50% of the share of these projects). These grant funds are tied to disaster declarations and are limited to 10% of the federal share of the public assistance monies made available.

Between 1989 (since authorization) and 1992, FEMA has approved 206 applications for hazard mitigation grants, obligating approximately $43 million. As Table 5.5 indicates, these funds have been used to finance a variety of different types of mitigation, including public/

TABLE 5.5

Rank of Project Categories by Percentage of Estimated Obligations (January 1989–August 1992)

Type of projects	$ Millions	Percentage
1. Public/private facilities	24.8	58
2. Drainage projects	5.9	14
3. Equipment purchases	5.3	12
4. Relocation of structures	4.7	11
5. Planning products	1.0	3
6. Education and training	0.5	1
7. Land improvements	0.5	1
TOTAL	42.7	100

Source: Joint Task Force on the Hazard Mitigation Grant Program (1992).

private facilities (e.g., floodproofing sewage treatment systems, seismic retrofitting), drainage projects, equipment purchases, relocation of structures, planning programs, education and training, and land improvements. Nearly 60% of the funds went for mitigation improvements to public/private facilities. It is perhaps somewhat discouraging that such a small percentage of these grants are for relocation/acquisition (about 11%) and planning programs (about 3%), which includes beach management plans, developing hazard mitigation plans, zoning and building code ordinances (see Joint Task Force on the Hazard Mitigation Grant Program , 1992).

A joint task force of the National Emergency Management Association and the Association of State Floodplain Managers was formed to evaluate the HMGP. This study identified a number of implementation programs and recommendations for addressing them. Among the concerns identified about the program were its slow pace of implementation, the lack of "hazard mitigation principles and guidance," difficulties in state-level coordination, and the failure of states and localities to identify mitigation opportunities before a disaster occurs. The specific recommendations of the joint task force include creating state teams to respond to disaster declarations; developing and endorsing a federal–state hazard mitigation strategy following each disaster declaration, which would identify mitigation opportunities; reinforcing preparation/update of state hazard mitigation plans through the federal-state agreement; and strengthening technical assistance activities (e.g., training and handbooks) and improving guidance on project eligibility (for a review of the full set of recommendations see Joint Task Force on the Hazard Mitigation Grant Program, 1992). Of special importance are the task force's conclusions that FEMA should better enforce state hazard mitigation plan requirements and seek to elevate the priority and importance given to these plans. As noted, land use/relocation/nonstructural programs are underrepresented in the HMGP, and overall the level of funding is quite modest.

The Stafford Act also made mitigation an eligible expense under the FEMA Public Assistance Program (and thus allowing for 75% federal contribution for reconstruction improvements to roads, bridges, utility lines, etc., which make them less vulnerable to future damage).

The existing federal disaster assistance framework does have some significant "teeth" in which to promote and require hazard mitigation. Section 409 states that FEMA may condition the provision of disaster assistance on state and local actions to mitigate hazards, "including safe land use and construction practices." In addition, states receiving disaster assistance are required to prepare a state hazard mitigation plan—a so-called Section 409 plan. These plans are intended to require states (and their localities) to seriously confront the natural hazards they are subject to and identify programs and policies which can be implemented to reduce them in the long run. In theory, FEMA can condition (and even withhold entirely) disaster assistance funds according to whether or not the programs and policies contained in the plan have actually been implemented. Politically, however, this is quite difficult to do, and FEMA has chosen not to adopt such a strident view toward the plans. On the positive side, most states required to prepare these plans have done so, though again after the disaster is over these plans are not necessarily implemented. Once the disaster is over, states are relieved of much of the pressure to undertake planning and mitigation activities, and FEMA lacks a clear system for monitoring state progress and compliance with 409 plans.

Another effort to coordinate the actions of these different agencies was the Interagency Hazard Mitigation agreement signed in 1980.

Under this agreement an interagency hazard mitigation team is called into action immediately following a disaster declaration and is required to prepare a report within 15 days of the declaration. These reports typically identify hazard mitigation opportunities and contain recommendations, many of which have been pursued by FEMA and other federal agencies. These recommendations also typically feed into the Section 409 hazard mitigation plan prepared by the state.

Coastal Barrier Resource Act

The Coastal Barrier Resources Act (CoBRA), enacted by Congress in 1982, represents an attempt to shift away from some of the ill-effects of federal subsidies such as flood insurance and disaster assistance. A product of conservative political times, CoBRA's stated objectives are to reduce growth pressures on undeveloped barrier islands; to reduce threats to people and property and to minimize the public expenditures that typically accompany such disasters; and to reduce damage to fish, wildlife, and other sensitive environmental resources.

The Act designated a Coastal Barrier Island Resources System (CBRS), originally comprised of 186 undeveloped barrier island units, including 453,000 acres and 666 miles of shoreline. After a certain date, a number of federal subsidies would no longer be permitted in these designated areas, including the issuance of new flood insurance policies; the expenditure of federal monies for roads, bridges, utilities, erosion control, etc.; and nonemergency forms of disaster relief. The Department of Interior has responsibility for implementing the program.

Barrier islands were defined in the Act as to include depositional geologic features (barrier islands, barrier spits) and "associated aquatic habitats" (e.g., adjacent marshes, estuaries; see P.C. 97-348; 16 U.S.C. 3501-10). Criteria for determining whether a barrier island unit was undeveloped, and thus should be included, were (Godschalk, 1987):

- less than one walled and roofed building per five acres of fastland

- absence of urban infrastructure (vehicle access, water supply, wastewater disposal, and electrical service to each lot)

- not part of a development of 100 or more lots

A minimum land area of one-quarter mile of oceanfront was also employed for designating units (extending back to the bay or soundside).

Maps were initially prepared by the Department of Interior in 1981, under the Omnibus Budget Reconciliation Act of that year. Congress, in consultation with landowners and others, modified the actual boundaries of units, initially reducing the oceanfront area covered by the CoBRA provisions. The CBRS was later expanded in 1990 under the Coastal Barrier Improvement Act to include 560 units and 1.3 acres and 1200 shoreline miles (GAO, 1992). In addition, under the 1990 Act, the Department of Interior was directed to map all undeveloped coastal barriers along the Pacific coast (to eventually be forwarded to Congress for inclusion in the CBRS).

Several studies have sought to evaluate the effectiveness of CoBRA at discouraging barrier island development. One of the first exploratory studies was conducted by Godschalk (1984; 1987). This pilot study assessed the viewpoints (through telephone interviews and mail surveys) of developers, government officials, and conservationists in three states (North Carolina, South Carolina, and Florida), and included several case studies as well (Topsail Island, N.C.; Hutchinson Island, Fla.). The results of the Godschalk study were mixed but raised serious questions about the effectiveness of CoBRA. These limited case studies showed that at least initially the loss of subsidies did serve to slow development. However, the cases also indicated that, especially for larger forms of development (e.g., condominiums and multi-family projects), developers would likely be able to find replacement insurance and would also be able to replace other subsidies (e.g., through state funding for bridge construction).

A 1990 study by the National Wildlife Federation examined aerial photographs to determine the extent of new development occurring after the enactment of CoBRA (Jones and Stolzenberg, 1990). Specifically, structures were analyzed for 157 barrier island units, encompassing about 95,000 acres of fastland. These results show that considerable development occurred following the enactment of CoBRA—the study counted some 594 additional (post-CoBRA) structures, or an increase of over 40%. The development activity was particularly high in certain states. Development in Florida accounted for about 52% of the total counted. Significant numbers of additional structures were also found in North Carolina, South Carolina, Alabama, Delaware, and Texas.

More recently, the U.S. General Accounting Office (GAO) undertook an assessment of CoBRA in 1992. Specifically, the GAO study examined 34 CBRS units (from the original 186), similarly comparing aerial photographs over time along with field visits and building permit data (GAO, 1992). Extensive interviews with agency personnel and a random sample of property owners to determine whether restrictions on flood insurance were being complied with were also components of the study. The resulting conclusions of this study are similar. Of the 34 units analyzed, the GAO found that nine had undergone new development since 1982. About 1,200 new residential units had been constructed in these nine units, and additional development is planned for the future.

Yet, the study also concluded that the CoBRA restrictions have had some positive effect:

> CBRA's prohibitions of new federal expenditures and financial assistance have slowed, delayed, or stopped development in some CBRS units. For example, the principal owner of the CBRS unit at Deer Island, Mississippi, told us that he could not proceed with his development plans without federal flood insurance and other forms of federal assistance. In an effort to proceed with plans to build about 160 condominium vacation cabins, a swimming pool, tennis courts, roads, and a marina, he has been trying to get the unit removed from the CBRS. He wants to develop the unit despite a history of hurricane damage that devastated previous structures on the island. (GAO, 1992, p. 17)

Despite the Act's ability to slow down and discourage development in some units, the study does conclude that further development is likely unless stronger controls are pursued. In the study's words:

> Additional future development in 9 of the 34 CBRS units included in our review is planned and likely to occur with or without federal financial assistance. Other CBRS units that are accessible and/or suitable for development and investment may undergo similar development. While the availability of accessible coastal land is limited, populations of

coastal areas are expected to increase by tens of millions by the year 2010. This population increase will further spur market demand, providing an incentive for developers, owners and investors to assume the risks associated with owning and building in these storm-prone areas. Stronger protective measures may be needed if further development is to be discouraged. (GAO, 1992, p.24)

The GAO study also uncovered other problems with CoBRA implementation. The study's random sample of property owners found that about 9% of them were able to obtain flood insurance even though they were ineligible under CoBRA. (These problems appear largely associated with write-your-own companies; see GAO, 1992, p. 26.) Also, the study identified problems with the certification process established to ensure that federal agencies comply with the Act, though it concludes that federal agencies generally are adhering to the restrictions.

These studies suggest that CoBRA has not stopped development pressures on undeveloped coastal barriers, though the withdrawal of federal subsidies has had some effect in discouraging new development there. These results might suggest several policy directions. Possible additional actions identified by GAO include the fee-simple or less-than-fee-simple (easement) acquisition of undeveloped barrier lands, although the study acknowledges the high cost of such a strategy. (Fee-simple acquisition involves purchasing full ownership, or the entire "bundle of rights"; less-than-fee-simple acquisition involves purchasing less-than-full ownership, or a partial interest in the land, typically the right to build or develop on all or a portion of the land.) Some studies in the past have argued that despite the high cost of acquisition, the public savings in the long term still justify such purchases (e.g., see Miller, 1989).

Jones and Stolzenburg (1990) recommend removal of the remaining forms of federal subsidy allowable under the current federal income tax code (casualty loss deductions, interest and property tax deductions for second homes, and accelerated depreciation for seasonal rental properties); prohibition of all loans made by federally insured banks and lending institutions (originally waived under Section 11 of CoBRA);

prohibition of federal block grants; and prohibition of federally funded projects occurring outside designated units, yet affecting them.

Beach Renourishment and Shoreline Protection

Significant subsidies have also been provided in the form of funding and technical assistance from federal and state agencies for flood control and oceanfront property protection. These subsidies have been provided both for the installation of "hard" devices, such as seawalls, revetments, groins, jetties, and breakwaters, and "soft" approaches, such as beach renourishment and dune building. At the federal level the U.S. Army Corps of Engineers has had primary responsibility for such programs.

Miller has estimated that the Corps spends about $11 million annually for beach nourishment on barrier islands and another $22 million on flood control projects, stabilization, and dredging activities (Miller, 1989). Federal cost sharing has ranged from 55 to 90% (federal share). There is, consistently, a major collective subsidy of such projects. States have also been active in assisting and subsidizing these shore protection efforts. A number of states now provide state funding, often through the issuance of bonds, for local renourishment programs (often in combination with federal subsidies). In South Carolina, for instance, the state legislature created a $10 million Beach Renourishment Fund, most of which went to funding emergency renourishment and dune-rebuilding projects following Hurricane Hugo (see Kana, 1990). The state of Maryland has provided substantial funding (some $60 million) under its Shore Erosion Control Program (SECP) for beach renourishment in Ocean City. Also under the SECP the state provides interest-free loans and technical assistance for shorefront property owners experiencing erosion problems, including construction of bulkheads and riprap (Pito, 1992). The state also provides 50% matching funds to property owners who undertake nonstructural erosion control (e.g., grass planting).

Beach renourishment remains a controversial approach to the coastal erosion problem. Such projects are very expensive (e.g., $5 million per mile in the case of Miami Beach) and have been shown to have much shorter lifespans than are typically estimated (e.g., see Pilkey and Clayton, 1987; Pilkey, 1989). A single northeaster or other significant coastal storm event can virtually single-handedly wipe out millions of dollars in renourishment expenditures (which is what has happened in Ocean City, Md.). A 1982 $5.2 million renourishment project in Ocean City, New Jersey, lasted only 2.5 months (Pilkey and Clayton, 1987). Coastal geologist Orrin Pilkey concluded from a major study of beach replenishment "We have found that for the last 25 years, coastal engineers have predicted the life time (and hence the cost) of replenished beaches with unvarnished and unjustified optimism. . . . Most replenished beaches last less than five years" (Pilkey, 1989, p.37).

Federal Clean Water Act

The federal Clean Water Act (CWA) contains several key programs and provisions which have had a substantial management influence on the coastal zone. These include a shared system of federal–state capitol of point sources, a nonpoint program, restrictions on discharges into wetlands (Section 404), and the National Estuary Program.

Section 404 Wetlands Restrictions   One of the most important sections of the federal Clean Water Act is Section 404, which represents the cornerstone of federal efforts to protect wetlands. Specifically, Section 404 restricts the discharge of dredge and fill materials into U.S. waters, requiring permit approval from the U.S. Army Corps of Engineers. The Corps must approve, deny, or modify such permit requests consistent with its own public interest review and the Section 404(b)(i) guidelines promulgated by EPA. (EPA also has final veto authority over the issuance of 404 permits.) Under the 404(b)(i) guidelines the Corps can issue a permit only where it concludes there are no practicable alternative sites for the proposed use (no-water-dependent uses are assumed to have practicable alternatives) and where impacts are mitigated to the maximum extent. Mitigation requirements can include the creation of new wetlands or the enhancement or restoration of degraded wetlands.

The 404 program has suffered from a number of problems and limitations, including a limited set of activities over which it has control (i.e., it only pertains to discharges), problems with conflicting definitions of wetlands, the perceived ease with which the Corps has issued permits (statistically, few permit requests are denied), the inconsistency with which wetlands mitigation and compensation are required, and the failure to designate in advance wetlands where discharges would and would not be appropriate. Much recent conflict has surrounded the regulatory definition of wetlands under the 404 program, and Congress has commissioned a study by the National Academy of Sciences to help resolve this issue; however, the resulting definition will likely address only what is a wetland and will not necessarily consider wetlands mitigation or movement in response to sea level rise.

The 404 program, then, does exercise considerable control over development in coastal areas. Clearly, however, the program could be strengthened in a number of ways which would permit it to more effectively reduce coastal risks and take into account future sea level rise. The land acquisition initiatives of the U.S. Fish and Wildlife Service (FWS), the National Park Service, and other agencies (e.g., through the Land and Water Conservation Fund, the Wetlands Resources Act, the Migratory Bird Conservation Act, and others) represent another potentially effective federal mechanism to regulate coastal development. Agencies such as FWS have, however, consistently fallen short of acquisition objectives, and the resources available for federal acquisition generally have been quite limited.

The National Estuarine Reserve Research System

The National Estuarine Reserve Research System (NERRS) was created by Section 315 of the Coastal Zone Management Act (CZMA) of 1972. The Secretary of Commerce was directed to "[a]cquire, develop, or operate estuarine sanctuaries, to serve as natural field laboratories in which to study and gather data on the natural and human processes occurring within the estuaries of the coastal zone" (16 U.S.C. §1461, 1972). The CZMA also created the system to "[a]cquire lands to provide access to public beaches and other public coastal areas of environmental, recreational, historical, aesthetic, ecological, or cultural value" (16 U.S.C. §1461, 1972).

These purposes were to fulfill the perceived need for more information regarding the functions and processes of estuarine ecosystems and humans' effects on them. The value of the nation's estuaries had been realized, but before the institution of NERRS fewer and fewer undisturbed or nonpolluted estuarine areas were available for scientific study and public education. Hence, the NERRS was established to create estuarine "field laboratories."

The NERRS is administered by the National Oceanic and Atmospheric Administration (NOAA), which in 1974 published guidelines for selection and management of sanctuaries and for the operation of the Estuarine Sanctuary Program (ESP), as it was originally titled. The NOAA guidelines contain a biogeographic classification system (BGC), defining 11 "types" of estuarine ecosystems. In 1981 a two-tiered approach for estuary selection was created; 27 biogeographical subcategories, or "regions," were added to the original 11 ecosystem definitions. This approach allowed for "regional differentiation" as well as ensured a "variety of ecosystems" for the program.

Funding of the NERRS operates on a 50/50 federal/state cost-share basis. Three types of matching grants are available to any state with laws that protect estuarine resources. These include (1) the preacquisition award, for site selection and preparation of draft management plans; (2) the acquisition and development award for land acquisition, minor construction activities (such as nature trails and boat ramps), and program development; and (3) the operation and management award, for assistance in implementing the research, educational, and administrative programs that are detailed in the individual research reserve management plans.

The National Marine Sanctuary Program

The National Marine Sanctuary Program (NMSP) was created in 1972 by Title III of the Marine Protection, Reserve and Sanctuary Act (MPRSA) and is administered by NOAA. The program was established to create and manage sanctuaries in areas of national significance in order to protect coastal and marine resources and to conduct scientific research in relatively pristine waters. Sites selected must exhibit qualities of a unique ecological, historical, research, educational, recreational, or aesthetic nature.

Eleven marine sanctuaries have been designated thus far, including U.S.S. Monitor (N.C.); Gray's Reef (Ga.); Flower Garden Banks (Tex./La.); Channel Islands, Gulf of the Farollones, and Monterey Bay (Calif.); Fagatele Bay, American Somoa; Florida Keys; Stellwagen Bank (Mass.); and Hawaii Humpback Whale Sanctuary. These additional areas are expected to be designated in the near future: Thunder Bay (Mich.); Norfolk Canyon (Va.); and Olympic Coast and North Puget Sound (Wash.)

The stated policies of MPRSA (16 U.S.C. §1431) are to

- Identify areas of the marine environment of national significance due to their resource or human use value

- provide authority for comprehensive and coordinated conservation and management of these marine areas that will complement existing regulatory authorities

- support, promote, and coordinate scientific research and monitoring of the resources of these marine areas

- enhance public awareness, understanding, appreciation and wise use of the marine environment

- facilitate, to the extent compatible with the primary objective of resource protection, all public and private uses of the resources of these marine areas not prohibited pursuant to other authorities

Within individual designated sanctuaries multiple use has been one of the most problematic and controversial policies. The reserve must be carefully designed and managed so that human activity in the sanctuary does not adversely impact preservation and conservation efforts. The concept of multiple use was introduced to accommodate the various activities that are demanded of the sanctuary's resources. These include activities such as recreational and commercial fishing, scuba diving, vessel traffic, and oil exploration and drilling. By allowing sanctuaries to be used for purposes other than research, the designation of some areas was made more politically and economically feasible. However, national reserves are managed in such a way that there are no "zoning" regulations within each sanctuary; a particular use is either permitted throughout the park or prohibited completely. Therefore, areas within the sanctuary that are especially fragile, such as estuaries or coral reefs, may be subjected to damaging activities.

Another problem facing the NMSP is the enforcement and jurisdictional mechanisms in place. There is a multiplicity of agencies at all levels of government with regulatory authority within each designated sanctuary, and a lack of coordination and cooperation has been experienced at some sites.

For instance, in addition to NOAA, the National Marine Fisheries Service has authority to enforce regulations at all sanctuaries; the

National Park Service and various state agencies are also often involved in regulatory enforcement. Conflict has been known to arise between the various agencies involved. However, there has been a concerted effort at intergovernmental coordination on some levels. The Coast Guard and NOAA, for example, are directed to coordinate enforcement activities in designated sanctuaries. Furthermore, since the 1992 reauthorization and amendments, NOAA now has the power to review all federal agency actions which impact on the sanctuaries.

Public participation and education are two important aspects of the NMSP. The educational programs accompanying some sanctuaries have been especially successful. Members of the public, including many school children, have been made aware of the value of our marine resources, the fragility of marine ecosystems, and the threats that they face. Public education has also tended to bolster protection and enforcement efforts.

Local citizens are encouraged to participate in the NMSP at all stages. The selection and designation process is open to public comment, and citizens and other interested parties are allowed to give testimony regarding plans that have been proposed by NOAA. Public steering or advisory committees for long-term sanctuary management have also been proposed. While public participation has played an important role in the NMSP, there have been some drawbacks; in some instances the NMSP designation and selection process has become cumbersome and lengthy due to prolonged and protracted debate.

Critics of the NMSP have pointed out that the program can never reach its stated goals given the limited funding it receives. The selection and designation of new sanctuaries is lengthy and requires many staff hours to prepare the extensive environmental impact statements, management plans, and resource assessment documents required. Furthermore, operation of existing sanctuaries requires financial support for educational programs, regulatory enforcement, and sanctuary maintenance. Unlike the National Estuarine Reserve Research System, the NMSP does not operate on a cost-share budget with the states; federal funds must cover all the financial needs of the NMSP.

While funding for the NMSP has increased over time with the inclusion of more sanctuaries, there are limited opportunities for growth of the program at current funding levels. In fact, as the number of sanctuaries has increased, federal dollars spent per square nautical miles has actually decreased. Although the 1992 reauthorization of the NMSP increased funding significantly, future designations will necessarily spread the available monies that much more thinly.

Critics of the NMSP have also pointed out that the designation of individual, relatively small areas of the ocean as sanctuaries does not provide adequate protection for those areas or for the ocean as a whole. Designated sanctuaries are not immune to external forces such as oil spills, nearby dredge spoils, intensive fish and shellfish harvesting, and other events which impact the health of the resources within sanctuary borders.

The program has no mechanism for regulating such activities beyond jurisdictional boundaries, and as a result cannot safeguard the area. However, despite these criticisms, the NMSP has thus far provided an effective management framework for preserving some of our nation's most unique and valuable natural marine resources.

The Florida Keys National Marine Sanctuary has incorporated some innovative techniques into its management plan. The Florida Keys National Marine Sanctuary and Protection Act was enacted by Congress in 1990. According to the Act, the Key Largo and Looe Key National Marine Sanctuaries, established in 1975 and 1981, respectively, were incorporated into the new Florida Keys Sanctuary. The sanctuary is now the second largest of its kind in the United States, encompassing approximately 2,800 square nautical miles.

The Act lays out certain rules for the sanctuary, including restricting commercial vessel traffic within an internationally designated "area to be avoided." In addition, the large size of the new sanctuary affords the opportunity to set up differing regulations for separate areas within its borders, similar to a system already in place at the Great Barrier Reef Marine Park of Australia. A system of zones with varying levels of restrictions to ensure protection of resources is incorporated into the comprehensive management plan for the sanctuary. Some areas can continue to be used in the accustomed ways, while other areas can be designated for preservation, restoration, or scientific research. This system provides for multiple uses within the sanctuary while also making certain its resources are protected for the future (Florida Department of Natural Resources).

Other Federal Influences

There are a number of other federal programs and policies which can be seen to influence coastal development patterns. Clearly, coastal growth has been subsidized by a variety of federal development programs and grants, many of them serving as impetus for the enactment of CoBRA. The Farmers Home Administration, for example, provides subsidies in the form of community facility loans, business/industry loans, and rural housing loans (e.g., see GAO, 1992, Appendix III). The Department of Housing and Urban Development provides guaranteed home loans, as does the Department of Veterans Affairs; the Rural Electrification Administration provides loans for development of electrical systems; the U.S Environmental Protection Agency has provided extensive funding for wastewater treatment and water systems; and the Department of Transportation has provided extensive funding for the construction of highways, roads and bridges, and other improvements which have served to make many otherwise remote coastal areas readily accessible. Most of these development-related grants and subsidies are not coastal-specific, and estimates of their magnitude and actual impacts in coastal regions are difficult to come by.

Coastal development subsidies are also provided in the form of tax expenditures, or deductions, and other subsidies contained in federal and state tax codes. Several major tax code subsidies have been provided at the federal level. The casualty loss deduction allows coastal property owners to deduct the cost of uninsured damages resulting from hurricanes and other natural disasters. Allowable deductions are determined by subtracting the post-storm value of property from its prestorm value, less insurance received. The deduction is only allowed where losses exceed 10% of adjusted gross income.

Other federal tax code subsidies include interest and property tax deductions for second homes (where much coastal development has been) and accelerated depreciation for seasonal rental properties. In large degree these types of subsidies are hidden, and estimates of their aggregate cost are hard to come by. There is little doubt, however, that the extent of these public costs is substantial.

Conclusions

This chapter has briefly reviewed several of the primary federal programs, laws, and policies which influence the coastline. The federal Coastal Zone Management Act (CZMA) was introduced here; the state programs initiated under the CZMA are discussed in Chapter 6.

This review of key programs and laws leads to several important conclusions about federal coastal policy in the United States. First, as the review indicates, policy is fragmented and dispersed over several different federal agencies and departments. There is no single federal agency in charge of coordinating these different programs and laws and no comprehensive, unified national coastal management plan or program. Moreover, the review of programs illustrates that federal policy can and does influence the coast and coastal development in numerous ways. Historically, the federal government has provided a number of different subsidies to coastal development, including making available federally subsidized flood insurance, disaster assistance monies, income tax code provisions (e.g., casualty loss deductions), and a host of infrastructure subsidies (e.g., funding for roads and highways, sewage treatment plants). At the same time, the federal government has sought to promote conservation and protection of coastal resources, for instance, by acquiring coastal areas for national seashores and wildlife refuges and encouraging coastal states and localities to prepare coastal management plans. We would argue that many of the federal subsidies should be eliminated or substantially reduced if sensible and sustainable coastal development is to be achieved. Coastal property owners should be asked to assume, as close as possible, the full costs of locating where they choose. This suggests, for example, the need to substantially raise NFIP premiums, to curtail the issuance of new flood insurance in especially risky locations (e.g., within V zones, seaward of a 30- or 50-year erosion line), to curtail or substantially reduce post-disaster assistance, and to modify the U.S. tax code so that it encourages rather than discourages sensible development patterns.

Many of these federal programs and policies are not without certain management benefits. As a result of the NFIP, development occurring within the 100-year floodplain must adhere to certain positive mitigative building standards (e.g., elevation and floodproofing). The federal CZMA has clearly resulted in the enactment of state and local management controls that would not have otherwise been undertaken. As a result of Section 404 of the CWA many thousands of acres of coastal wetlands have received substantial protection from development. Under the Stafford Act, many states have prepared hazard mitigation plans which may serve to substantially reduce risk levels in coastal areas in the future.

This review has shown, moreover, that there are substantial management teeth in many of the federal programs identified. Federal Disaster Assistance provisions, for instance, contain substantial authority for FEMA to require that more attention be paid to hazard mitigation by states and localities. Programs such as the Section 1362 Flooded Properties Purchase Program make considerable sense from a long-term loss-reduction perspective and could be expanded. Provisions of the federal CWA (especially Section 404) have the potential, if stringently and conscientiously enforced, to reduce coastal hazards and to further minimize coastal environmental degradation. Many of these programs, then, while perhaps not as directed toward management and mitigation in their present forms, do constitute a positive foundation on which to build a more effective and sensible federal coastal management strategy or plan.

What is perhaps most obvious in this quick review is the lack of a national coastal management *plan* or *strategy* and the lack of a mechanism for coordinating these many different federal programs and policies. The federal Coastal Zone Management Act (and the Office of Ocean and Coastal Resource Management within NOAA) is the closest thing to such a comprehensive strategy, but as we have seen, it has many limitations and does not, in fact, serve to effectively coordinate these different federal programs.

6

State Coastal
Management Programs

As Chapter 5 illustrates, there are numerous federal programs and agencies which have some influence on coastal development, but no single agency or strategy. Moreover, historically in the United States context, land use control and planning (including coastal areas) are powers left to states and localities. In 1972, with the passage of the Coastal Zone Management Act (CZMA), the federal government initiated a new era of partnership with states to promote planning and management of the nation's coastlines. In this chapter we will review the content and focus of state coastal management programs under the CZMA, with profiles of certain states that have undertaken especially innovative or successful approaches.

As described in Chapter 5, under CZMA, funds are provided on a cost-share basis to states to develop and implement their own coastal management programs. These state programs must meet certain minimum requirements and must be approved by the Department of Commerce (specifically the Office of Ocean and Coastal Resource Management). Once approved, all subsequent federal actions and policies must be consistent with these state programs to the maximum extent practicable. Thus, the CZMA provides states with the double incentive of financial assistance and greater control over federal actions and policies.

The incentives provided under CZMA have encouraged a high degree of state participation. Twenty-nine of 35 eligible coastal and Great Lakes states and American territories now have federally approved coastal plans, with other states such as Texas and Georgia in the process of preparing programs. While in some cases the CZMA has provided funding for states to undertake management activities they would have undertaken in any event, most observers believe the Act has done much to encourage states to better plan for and manage their shorelines. There is little doubt that the Act has resulted in greater levels of protection for wetlands and estuarine waters, less risky coastal development patterns, and generally greater levels of state and local planning of development and growth.

One of the key features of the CZMA is the flexibility coastal states have in crafting their plans to meet their own unique or special circumstances and political and cultural contexts. There is, consequently, considerable variation among the state programs in terms of the organization of their management programs and the types of management tools and techniques employed. Some states had little in the way of a management framework prior to 1972. In North Carolina, for instance, enactment of the Coastal Area Management Act (CAMA) created an entirely new regulatory and planning framework, including the creation of the Coastal Resources Commission (CRC), a permitting system for activities in areas of environmental concern, and mandated local coastal planning. Prior to CAMA neither the state nor local governments exercised much direct control over development in coastal areas.

Other coastal states have taken a "networking" approach, in which their coastal programs involved a pulling together of a number of largely pre-existing laws and management programs. Coastal states exhibiting this pattern include Florida, Wisconsin, Massachusetts, Maine, and Oregon.

In some states the coastal management program has been integrated into a much broader state-planning framework. Oregon is perhaps the best example of this approach. Here coastal management requirements are expressed in the form of several statewide goals—part of a set of 19 statewide goals which serve as the basis for a system of statewide land use planning. Local government plans and state agency actions must be consistent with these goals. In other states, coastal management is not well integrated in broader statewide planning. In North Carolina, for instance, the CAMA program applies only to the coastal zone and has little relationship to planning in other parts of the state.

States have also taken different approaches to defining the coastal zone to which regulations and program requirements apply. In North Carolina, the 20 counties which border the ocean comprise the coastal zone; in Rhode Island, the coastal zone boundary extends 200 feet inland of a coastal feature; and in Connecticut, the coastal zone includes all lands within the interior contour elevation of the 100-year frequency flood zone, or a 1,000-foot setback from the mean high-water mark, or a 1,000-foot setback from the inland boundary of mapped tidal wetlands, whichever is farthest inland.

Not all state coastal management programs have experienced complete success. Two main trouble areas continue to be implementation and enforcement of programs and regulations. For example, Florida's Coastal Management Program looks good on paper, but has suffered persistent implementation problems since its inception in 1978. The Florida program is fragmented by its very nature; it is a networked program, combining 26 laws and 17 agencies. The coordinating function is a difficult challenge, and no one agency has comprehensive responsibility and accountability for the state's coastal program. Furthermore, while Florida has strong requirements for local planning, the approved coastal elements of local plans are not enforced or overseen at the state level. While there are a number of strong, comprehensive and innovative natural resource management programs in Florida, without better cooperation between the various elements and more stringent enforcement mechanisms, the program will not live up to its full potential (Delaney et al., 1991).

Overview of State Programs

Part of the perceived desirability of CZMA is the freedom individual states have to craft their own unique coastal management programs to fit their particular physical, social, and political circumstances. Consequently there is considerable variation from state to state as to the actual components of the coastal management program. Several broad program categories can be identified, on which our quick overview will focus: local land use/comprehensive planning; shoreline management and retreat; restrictions to shore-hardening structures; coastal wetlands protection; managing reconstruction; unbuildable lots; sea level rise; beach access and land acquisition; building codes and construction standards; cumulative and secondary impacts; urban waterfront development, intergovernmental relationships; areas of particular concern, and ocean management.

Local Planning Requirements

Many state coastal management programs incorporate a local planning requirement. Prior to the enactment of the CAMA, for instance, coastal localities in North Carolina were not required to undertake basic comprehensive or land use planning. Under CAMA all 20 coastal counties were required to prepare local coastal plans by a certain date, consistent with state guidelines, which were reviewed and approved by the Coastal Resources Commission. Cities and towns in the coastal zone were given the option of preparing their own plans or having the county prepare them (most have chosen the former). All local Land Use Plans (LUPs) must be updated every five years.

CAMA guidelines require LUPs to address a number of issues, including resource protection and management, economic and community development, public participation, and intergovernmental coordination. The plan must also delineate the community's constraints to growth and development, both in terms of land suitability and carrying capacity. Storm hazard mitigation, post-disaster recovery, and evacuation plans are also an integral part of each CAMA land use plan. Furthermore, each jurisdiction must prepare a land use map which classifies land into such uses as developed, transition, rural, rural-with-services, and conservation.

Shoreline Management and Retreat

Many state coastal programs have as a major component the management and regulation of activities along ocean beachfronts or estuarine shores. As noted in earlier chapters, shoreline erosion is a significant problem along much of the U.S. coastline, and state coastal programs seek to minimize exposure to these hazards through a variety of means. States also must deal with the flooding and storm hazards associated with close proximity to the ocean, as well as the prospect of long-term sea level rise. Some states have characterized these measures in terms of the desire to engage in "strategic retreat" from the shoreline.

Probably one of the most effective ways of addressing erosion and other shoreline hazards, and of promoting coastal retreat, is through regulatory setback requirements. As Table 6-1 indicates, some 12 states now impose some form of coastal setback, requiring new development to locate a certain distance landward of the ocean as measured

TABLE 6.1

Status of State Setback Authorities

State or territory	Setback legislation	State or territory	Setback legislation
Maine	yes[a]	Louisiana	no
New Hampshire	no	Texas	no
Massachusetts	no	California	no
Rhode Island	yes	Oregon	no
Connecticut	no	Washington	no
New York	yes	Alaska	no
New Jersey	yes[b]	Ohio	no
Delaware	yes	Illinois	no
Pennsylvania	yes	Michigan	yes
Maryland	no	Wisconsin	no
Virginia	no	Minnesota	no
North Carolina	yes	Hawaii	yes
South Carolina	yes	American Samoa	no
Georgia	no	Northern Marianas	yes[a]
Florida	yes	Guam	no
Alabama	yes	Virgin Islands	yes[a]
Mississippi	no	Puerto Rico	yes[a]

Source: Houlahan (1989).

[a]State or territory has a construction setback, but it is not primarily for coastal erosion hazard purposes; see text for discussion.

[b]New Jersey setback line—the state setback only applies to projects requiring a state CAFRA permit (projects of greater than 24 residential units). Local municipalities have authority for sub-CAFRA projects through dune/beach protection ordinances.

from mean high water, first line of vegetation, and various other marks (Platt et al., 1992b; NRC, 1990; Houlahan, 1989). Increasingly these setback requirements are calculated according to local erosion rates. North Carolina, for example, employs one of the toughest erosion-based setbacks. Specifically, for small-scale development in beachfront areas, new development must be set back a distance of at least 30 times the average annual rate of erosion for that particular stretch of coastline, measured from the first stable line of vegetation (e.g., see N.C. Division of Coastal Management, 1988; Godschalk et al., 1989; Platt et al., 1992b). Development must also be landward of the crest of the "primary dune" and the landward toe of the "frontal dune." For larger structures, the setback is doubled to 60 times the rate of erosion.

Other types of shoreline restrictions are also imposed. Under New York's Coastal Erosion Hazard Areas Act, for example, in certain erosion zones (in so-called "structural hazard zones") only "moveable" structures are permitted (see Platt et al., 1992b). Specific density limitations are imposed by some states in certain high-risk locations. Under North Carolina's CAMA, for instance, development in inlet hazard zones is restricted to structures of less than 5,000 square feet in size, and generally must not exceed a density of more than one unit per 15,000 square feet of developable land (N.C. Division of Coastal Management, 1988).

Some state programs have sought to facilitate and promote landward relocation of structures. In response to rising Great Lakes levels, the state of Michigan created the Emergency Home Moving Program (EHMP). Under this program the state provides loan interest subsidies for property owners wishing to relocate lakefront structures subject to erosion (see Platt et al., 1992b; St. Amand, 1991). Two options were provided to property owners: either a 3% interest subsidy on the first $25,000 of relocation costs or a one-time grant of $3,500. As a condition of this assistance, property owners must move their structures at least 45 feet landward. The state has also implemented an Emergency Home Flood Protection Program, which provides similar subsidies for the elevation of threatened structures (see Platt et al., 1992b).

Many state coastal programs also impose some form of real estate disclosure requirement, which may be somewhat useful in discouraging hazardous shoreline development. Under North Carolina's CAMA permit program, for example, an applicant must sign an Area of Environmental Concern (AEC) Hazard Notice to acknowledge that "he or she is aware of the risks associated with development in the ocean hazard area and of the area's limited suitability for permanent structures" (N.C. Division of Coastal Management, 1988). Under South Carolina's modified beachfront management program similar disclosure provisions are required when a special beachfront variance is issued (see Beatley, 1992).

Restrictions to Shore-Hardening Structures

Some coastal states have also imposed significant restrictions on the building of erosion control structures (seawalls, revetments, groins, etc.). Some states, including North Carolina, South Carolina, and Maine, have banned the construction of new permanent shore-hardening structures altogether. Such actions serve in the long run to reduce destruction of beaches and put property owners on notice that should a beachfront structure end up subject to erosion hazards, it will not be permissible to construct such protective (yet damaging) structures. States like North Carolina have managed to resist recent political challenges to such controls.

Coastal Wetlands Protection

Most coastal states have also imposed restrictions on development in tidal or saltwater wetlands, and a smaller number apply restrictions to nontidal or freshwater wetlands. States typically require a permit before certain activities can take place in wetland areas, and usually include a more expansive list of such potentially damaging activities than those regulated under the federal Section 404 program (see below). Regulated activities typically include discharge of dredge and fill, draining of wetlands, and cutting of trees and destruction of vegetation, among others. Frequently these regulations extend to adjacent buffer areas as well. State wetland standards often incorporate many of the key concepts contained in the EPA 404(b)(i) guidelines, including restricting wetland alternatives to water-dependent uses and forbidding such activities where practicable alternatives exist.

Most state wetlands programs also require mitigation when natural wetlands are destroyed or damaged. Mitigation ratios imposed can be quite high, ranging from 2:1 to 7:1 (i.e., amount of created, restored, or enhanced acreage required for each acre of natural wetland destroyed or damaged). For a review of state wetland programs see Salvesen (1990).

Managing Reconstruction

Many state coastal programs also seek to manage rebuilding and reconstruction following hurricanes or other major flooding events. Most state programs require development permits for rebuilding substantially damaged structures. Hurricanes and coastal storm events, while exacting substantial human and economic cost, do often represent opportunities to rebuild and reconstruct in ways which minimize exposure to future risks (e.g., through relocation, setback requirements, elevation of buildings).

The South Carolina Beachfront Management Act (BMA), originally created in 1988, contained some of the most stringent reconstruction provisions in the country when Hurricane Hugo hit the coast a year later. In enacting the BMA, the state sought to explicitly implement a long-term shoreline retreat policy (flowing from the recommendation of a special blue-ribbon committee on beachfront management). Under the original BMA, habitable structures which were found to be "damaged beyond repair" (two-thirds or greater damaged) would only be allowed to rebuild landward of a no construction zone (the so-called "dead zone"). All structures rebuilt within a larger 40-year erosion zone were also required to move as far landward as possible. Some 159 beachfront structures located in the no construction zone were found to be damaged beyond repair (many of which would not have been able to rebuild at all under the Act). Pools and recreational amenities damaged 50% or greater were also prevented from being rebuilt. Restrictions were also placed on rebuilding erosion control structures if damaged greater than 50%. Vertical seawalls could be replaced with sloping revetments, but only under certain conditions. (For a discussion of the South Carolina Act, see Platt et al., 1992a; Beatley, 1992.) Opposition to the rebuilding restrictions following Hugo was intense, especially by beachfront property owners. Several takings decisions (e.g., *Lucas v. South Carolina Coastal Council*), moreover, suggested that the state's financial liability in cases where the dead zone restrictions prevented all reasonable use of a parcel could exceed $100 million. These political dynamics led to a substantial softening of the law, completely eliminating the dead zone and creating a special variance procedure allowing development to occur even further seaward under certain conditions (seaward of the baseline, or the crest of the ideal dune). Despite creating somewhat stronger rebuilding restrictions for erosion control devices, the 1990 revisions in many ways represent a political retreat from retreat (for a discussion of these dynamics see Beatley, 1992).

It is worth noting that, increasingly, state coastal programs are requiring that local governments prepare hurricane and coastal storm recovery and reconstruction plans. North Carolina was the first state to impose such requirements, but other states have followed suit (e.g., Florida and South Carolina).

Unbuildable Lots

The 1992 Supreme Court case *Lucas v. South Carolina Coastal Council* is one all coastal managers and planners should be cognizant of due to its ramifications for regulatory takings of private property. But a taking does not occur until a disgruntled landowner takes the regulatory official or agency to court, claiming loss of property rights because of an oceanfront setback rule or other similar regulation. Coastal planners and managers must therefore be aware of *potential* takings claims *before* they reach the point of adjudication. Such caution is especially called for when coastal regulations create "unbuildable lots," such as occurred in the *Lucas* case.

In the *Lucas* case, the landowner alleged a South Carolina regulation had effected an unconstitutional taking of his oceanfront lots. The statute concerned was the 1988 South Carolina Beachfront Management Act, which established an oceanfront setback line and prohibited the construction of any habitable structures seaward of that line. The U.S. Supreme Court held that any regulation which prohibited a landowner from making any "economically beneficial or productive use of his property" constituted a categorical taking which required compensation, unless the government could prove that the regulation prohibited activities which would be considered a nuisance (i.e., a threat to human health, welfare, or safety arising from "unreasonable, unwarranted or unlawful use by a person of his own property"—*Black's Law Dictionary.*)

One of the reasons the Court found that Mr. Lucas had no economically beneficial use left to his property after the application of the setback rule may be that the South Carolina rule prohibited Mr. Lucas from building almost any type of structure at all on his lot. Only a small walkway or deck would have been permissible, although Mr. Lucas had originally intended to build a single-family residence.

Other states have approached this situation differently than South Carolina. The North Carolina Coastal Area Management Act (CAMA), for instance, allows a wider range of structures to be built seaward of the oceanfront setback. These uses include camp grounds, unpaved parking areas, outdoor tennis courts, elevated decks of a certain size, some types of beach accessways, unhabitable gazebos and sheds of proscribed square footage, temporary amusement stands, and swimming pools.

States have taken a variety of approaches to the unbuildable lots situation. In 1986, the North Carolina Division of Coastal Management (DCM) inventoried all the beachfront vacant lots which were rendered unbuildable due to setback regulations. The owners of the lots were informed that their applications for building permits might be denied, and that DCM was willing to offer between $200 to $5,000 for each lot. The vacant lots would be used to construct public beach access facilities (Ballenger, 1993).

Public reaction to the offer of purchase was mixed. Some owners were interested in the offer, while others, shocked to discover that they might be prohibited from constructing any habitable structures, were quite irate (Ballenger, 1993).

Although lots may be stripped of their value as residential property, some have argued that economic value still remains in unbuildable lots. For instance, adjacent landowners may wish to purchase the property in order to construct walkways, decks, or beach cabanas; provide a drain field for a septic tank; or obtain additional parking space. In addition, landowners fearing the state purchase of the property in order to provide public beach access could bring an "onslaught of the unwashed masses" might purchase adjacent unbuildable lots precisely to forestall such a possibility. Or, alternatively, owners of motels and multi-family structures not located on the oceanfront might purchase such lots in order to provide beach access for their guests or lessees (Ballenger, 1993).

Many states which have instituted oceanfront setback requirements include variance or exemption provisions. Michigan, for instance, has a system for granting exceptions for construction on substandard lots. Special permits are issued with conditions that structures be made readily movable and that all structures be relocated before shoreline erosion damage occurs. The landowner must further agree to follow property engineering standards in design, to use a septic system located landward of the structure rather than a sanitary sewer, and to locate the structure as far landward as the local zoning ordinance will permit, among other provisions (Ballenger, 1993).

The state of Florida allows for a variance under certain circumstances. Single-family homes may be constructed seaward of the setback line if the land was platted before the setback regulations came into effect. However, the landowner may not receive a variance if he owns another parcel adjacent to the parcel he is attempting to build on. An exception will not be granted under the Florida regulations if the structure will be built seaward of the frontal dunes (Ballenger, 1993).

North Carolina CAMA also contains a variance provision, whereby permission to use land in a manner otherwise prohibited by the regulations will be granted if the landowner can show "practical difficulties or unnecessary hardships." The applicant must further show that the difficulties or hardships result from conditions which are peculiar to the property and which could not reasonably have been anticipated when the rules were adopted.

Despite the presence of variance provisions in setback laws, if few to no variances are actually granted, landowners who have been deprived of all practical use of their property may still have grounds to bring a regulatory takings claim to court. On the one hand, there is a delicate balance between drafting setback regulations which create lots so unbuildable that the courts will find no "economically beneficial or productive use" of the property remains and thus entail a regulatory taking requiring compensation and, on the other, avoiding regulations that are so broad in their exceptions that nearly all property owners are eventually permitted to build inappropriate structures on oceanfront lots. Coastal managers and planners who are well-versed in the *Lucas* perils that are possible in setback cases may well be able to avoid takings claims through careful preparation and drafting.

Sea Level Rise

Some states have also begun to explicitly incorporate consideration of sea level rise into their programs. Klarin and Hershman (1990) report that 17 coastal states have officially recognized the problem of sea level rise and have undertaken assessments of the problem/issue (e.g., through proclamations, legislative findings, research and impact assessments). Eleven coastal states have initiated new public and intergovernmental processes (e.g., forming a sea level rise task force or a policy-setting process), and 13 states already have existing regulations adaptable (or partially adaptable) to future sea level rise (e.g., coastal setbacks, such as those discussed above). Klarin and Hershman report, however, that only three states have adopted new policies specifically to respond to sea level rise. Under Maine's Coastal Wetlands Act, wetland buffer zones are established to anticipate migration in response to sea level rise. As this zone moves in the future, development within it must also move (specifically, development must be relocated or abandoned if it encroaches for more than a six-month period or if damaged 50% or more). Also, in certain frontal dune areas (where some development is permitted), developers are required to build structures (those exceeding a certain minimum size) to take into account a three-foot rise in sea levels over the next 100 years (see Klarin and Hershman, 1990).

Beach Access and Land Acquisition

Nearly all coastal states are grappling with the issue of public access to the shoreline. Although effective demand for recreational shoreline areas is at an all-time high, there is an ever-dwindling supply of lake, ocean, and other waterfront property available and accessible to the public. Increased private ownership of shorefront property has fenced off many of these places and literally barred people from gaining access to them. There is a delicate balance between providing enough public access so that all residents and visitors can enjoy the beach, and protecting the rights of owners whose property is adjacent to the public beach area.

Many state coastal management programs are addressing problems of public access through a wide range of activities, including regulatory, statutory, and legal systems; innovative techniques to acquire, improve, and maintain access sites; coastal public access management plans that target all users and resources of recreational, historical, aesthetic, ecological, and cultural value; and protection measures that minimize the potential adverse impacts of access on coastal natural resources and private property (U.S. Department of Commerce, 1992).

In some states common-law doctrine establishes more extensive public rights to beach access. In Texas, for instance, under the doctrine of customary use the public beach extends landward to the natural line of vegetation, thus encompassing much of the dry beach as well as the wet. The 1959 Texas Open Beaches Act codifies this common law and reinforces the public's right of access to the coastline. Texas law was tested in 1983 when, following Hurricane Alicia, a number of beach-front property owners on Galveston Island were prevented by the Texas Attorney General's office from rebuilding because their structures had become situated on the public beach. Because the extent of the public beach is determined by the first line of vegetation, and because this line moves in response to storms and other natural coastal processes, the public right in Texas amounts to a rolling easement. When Alicia moved the natural line of vegetation landward, homes that prior to the storm were on private beach, were now on the public beach. Several property owners challenged the constitutionality of the Texas law, claiming that the actions of the Attorney Generals office to prevent rebuilding amounted to an unconstitutional taking of property. The Texas Supreme Court, however, found in favor of the state, upholding the state's restrictions on rebuilding.

One principle means of securing access to the shoreline for the public is by attaching conditions to permits issued by the government for development. Permits are granted only if the developer of shorefront property agrees to set aside a prescribed area for the public to use as an accessway. A recorded fee, easement, or deed restriction can assure long-term public access for the specified area.

Developers and prospective buyers are often not convinced of the fairness of such conditions. However, the logical and legal rationale for requiring shoreline access is not a radical or new concept. In some states, for example, under the Public Trust Doctrine the oceans have always been considered a public resource. In order to effectively make use of this resource, the public must have ready access to it. Private property owners cannot bar the way to public property.

However, despite the generally solid legal background, there are legal obstacles to requiring the provision of public access as a condition for development permits. One major obstacle lies in the Fifth Amendment to the U.S. Constitution (the takings clause). The Constitution requires that there be the proper "nexus" between the impact of the development and the conditions imposed.

This point was made clear in 1987 by the U.S. Supreme Court in *Nollan v. California Coastal Commission*, 107 S.Ct. 3141 (1987). In *Nollan*, the Supreme Court majority, in an opinion by Justice Scalia, held that a condition attached to a permit must "substantially advance" a legitimate governmental interest, and the governmental interest must be the same one served by the permit itself. The facts of the case are simple. The Nollans owned a dilapidated bungalow on the California coast which they wanted to demolish, remove, and replace with a new and larger house. They applied to the California Coastal

Commission for a permit. The permit was granted on one condition: the Nollans were required to convey to the public a lateral access easement over their beachfront between their new house and the shoreline. The easement would allow the public to walk across their beachfront between the mean high tide and a pre-existing sea wall. The Nollans sued, claiming a taking without just compensation.

The Coastal Commission's defense was that the lateral easement was necessary to provide the public with views of the ocean and to help overcome the "psychological barrier" that existing development had in effect created.

The Supreme Court held that this was a taking, emphasizing the character of the governmental action: physical occupation. The Court said it could not find the required nexus or close fit between the condition imposed and the governmental interest to be furthered, since people already on the beach (these were the only people who could have made use of any lateral access easement on the beachfront side of the house) did not need any encouragement to view the ocean. Justice Scalia found that a taking had occurred because the Nollans had lost the right to exclude others from their land.

Land use regulators will do well to heed the lessons of *Nollan*. The Supreme Court implied through the case that people have a right to build on their land, and that permits are not to be considered governmental benefits. Beyond this dicta, however, the specific *Nollan* requirement is not that difficult: permit conditions must relate directly to impacts caused by development.

Another coastal management strategy which some states are using is acquisition of coastal lands. Some states use acquisition to provide beach access, while other states put the land to other uses, such as safeguarding important habitats or preservation of especially sensitive ecological areas.

Although there may be problems associated with public acquisition of coastal lands, such as the limited funds available or the reluctance of some landowners to sell, acquisition is often the most appropriate, effective, and sometimes the only way to ensure large land areas can be added to the inventory of public accessways or conservation areas.

Acquisition can be in the form of fee simple (outright ownership) or less-than fee simple. While fee-simple acquisition is the most complete form of ownership and affords the public a right to use the land in any legal manner, it can also be expensive. Less-than-fee-simple rights can often provide the public with the right of use that is needed for that particular parcel, while the owner retains certain other rights in the property.

Easements are a very useful form of less-than-fee acquisition. An easement is the right to use someone else's land in some specifically designated manner. Easements are generally purchased in circumstances in which it is unnecessary or infeasible to purchase the land itself, that is, in which only some rights to use the land, such as the right to pass over it (e.g., for an accessway) are needed. Conservation easements can also be granted by a landowner, whereby the land will be reserved for conservation purposes and the owner agrees not to put the property to any incompatible use. Future owners are also subject to the terms of the easement. Landowners can often be persuaded to grant easements because of the tax consequences involved, including a decrease in the valuation of their property for property tax purposes.

Leaseholds are another commonly used less-than-fee acquisition technique. The owner of a parcel of land (lessor) grants an interested party (lessee) the right to use the land in a specified manner for a limited period of time. The leasehold thus creates and transfers to the lessee restricted rights, generally referred to as the leasehold estate, and reserves to the lessor all remaining property rights, known as the fee estate.

While leases are most frequently utilized as a legal instrument for the renting of buildings and structures, they can be applied to any number of other uses, including the provision of farming rights, public fishing and hunting rights on private lands, and public access across someone's property.

Another type of less-than-fee property interest is development rights. Among the "sticks" in the proverbial "bundle of sticks" which comprise the fee-simple absolute title to a piece of property is the right to develop the property for whatever purposes one wishes, within the confines of the local zoning laws. Public purchase of the owner's right to develop the property for certain purposes has been used to prevent the destruction or substantial transformation of historic structures, and to prevent the residential or commercial development of certain large open lands.

Development rights may be purchased outright by a public entity and "banked" in a charitable conservation trust or they may be purchased by a private developer and used to increase the density in a designated section of an urban area where, typically, the right to develop at greater than normal densities is extremely valuable to private developers. This latter method is commonly referred to as transfer of development rights (TDR).

Florida's Conservation and Recreation Lands (CARL) is one of the nation's most aggressive acquisition programs. Critical coastal resources and sensitive ecosystems have been protected throughout the state, and public access has been provided in some areas.

Another state-level entity that has been at the forefront of using acquisition for resource management is the California State Coastal Conservancy. The Conservancy was created in 1976 by the California legislature to allow the state to use acquisition as well as regulation for coastal protection, restoration, and management. The Coastal Conservancy has been especially effective in its use of innovative acquisition techniques, including less-than-fee interests and development rights transfers (including TDR and transfer of development credits, or TDC).

Many of these approaches were first initiated in response to funding constraints; it was soon discovered that less-than-fee ownership was just as satisfactory, or more so, for securing coastal resources. The Conservancy has been particularly creative in using various acquisition approaches as a part of broader program and project implementation efforts. For instance, the Conservancy has used less-than-fee methods in conjunction with fee acquisition, lot consolidation, and area planning programs.

The Conservancy has acted as a temporary repository for property interests attained and has also acted along with nonprofit land trusts and/or local governments. This flexibility and adaptability is one of the reasons for the Coastal Conservancy's many successes in California resource management (Grenell, 1988).

Building Codes and Construction Standards

Building codes and construction standards represent another important component of many state and local risk-reduction strategies (though not necessarily an explicit component of a state's coastal program). Coastal structures can be designed to better withstand hurricane winds, wave, and surge. Building codes may be state mandated (as in North Carolina) or local option (as in South Carolina) and can vary substantially in their stringency. The federal CZMA does not mandate that states impose building codes, and in some 12 coastal states adoption of building codes is left as a local option. It is not uncommon for rural areas especially to be without construction standards (see Manning, 1988). The stringency of the wind design standard to which coastal structures must be built is a variable. Under the North Carolina Building Code, for instance, construction on the Outer Banks must be designed to withstand wind speeds of 120 mph. Buildings there must also adhere to fairly stringent piling and foundation standards. The benefits of North Carolina's standards have been well illustrated by a study by Rogers et al. (1988), comparing damages from Hurricanes Alicia and Diana in Texas and North Carolina, respectively. Though the storms were comparable in strength and wind speeds, resulting damages were much less in North Carolina. The authors attribute the lower damages to North Carolina's mandatory construction standards and to the lack of any major control over building in the unincorporated areas of Texas (see National Committee on Property Insurance, 1988). While the South Florida Building Code (SFBC) is considered one of the strongest prescriptive codes anywhere (and similarly mandates a 120-mph wind-speed standard), post-storm damage inspections following Hurricane Andrew have identified a number of potential deficiencies in this code (e.g., poor performance of roof coverings, poor connection of roof systems, use of staples to attach plywood sheathing, problems with windows and wall siding; see Perry et al., 1992). Local enforcement and building compliance problems have also been implicated. Even though the SFBC is a relatively strong code, some have argued for even tougher standards given the location and the frequency and potential magnitude of future storm events (e.g., higher wind load standards).

Cumulative and Secondary Impacts

Many, if not most, coastal states are experiencing rapid growth and development along the shoreline. Not only are oceanfront properties being built, but as land costs skyrocket and the demand for waterfront or water-view property ever increases, other coastal areas are now being exploited, such as sounds, estuaries, and even wetlands. Not only do states have to face the challenge of dealing with the pressures on the natural environment caused by the new development itself, but the cumulative and secondary impacts of growth are becoming increasingly apparent. Cumulative impacts occur when activities which alone may not create significant changes in the environment are added together, producing a much larger effect over time. Secondary impacts occur when roads, bridges, municipal water and sewer facilities, and other construction takes place in the coastal zone, paving the way for more and/or increased density of development in the vicinity of the services provided.

The areas most vulnerable to cumulative and secondary impacts are generally those where growth is occurring most rapidly and where particularly sensitive natural resources are located. Many states, however, currently lack sufficient information on which to base an assessment of cumulative and secondary impacts, an important first step in measuring and controlling the impacts. With this in mind, some states have included significant projects in their coastal management programs designed to address cumulative and secondary impacts.

For instance, Florida is planning to use federal CZMA Section 309 Enhancement Grants monies to control the widespread and high-density use of on-site sewage disposal systems in subdivisions that have been "vested" under Florida law. Dense concentrations of these systems can cause contamination of groundwater and surface water and, in turn, of the state's coastal waters. The state will expand regulatory authority over septic systems to address concerns about the environmental quality of coastal waters and the public health consequences of degraded waters (U.S. Department of Commerce, 1992).

Urban Waterfront Development

A wide range of activities has been undertaken by coastal towns and cities in efforts to develop and redevelop their waterfront districts. Specific projects that have been carried out in several communities as a result of the implementation of revitalization plans include construction of marinas; docks; piers for commercial and recreational fishermen; boat ramps; retail, office, restaurant, and condominium complexes; and public access facilities. For instance, in Ponce and San Juan, Puerto Rico, docking facilities for cruise ships are being improved; while in Reedsport, Oregon, moorage for antarctic research vessels has been designed.

Many state coastal management programs have contributed to local communities' urban waterfront development efforts through grants of financial and technical assistance. Some localities have joined with one another and with the state coastal management program in a collaborative effort to revitalize an entire waterfront area. In New York, the state has established the Horizon's Waterfront Commission to develop a regional development plan for the entire Erie County waterfront. Representing municipalities, the county, and the state, the Commission has bonding authority and eminent domain powers to implement its plan.

Many states are reporting substantial private and public investment taking place in and around refurbished urban waterfronts. For instance, coastal management program funds were used in Kewaunee, Wisconsin, to plan and construct a 150-slip marina and waterfront park; the development catalyzed significant private investment in the area, in addition to attracting over 100,000 tourists annually. In Jersey City, New Jersey, a waterfront park and pier project was recently completed, and $2 billion in new construction condominiums and retail shops now surround the new park. The Malaloa Bulkhead project in American Samoa has opened the door for four new marine-dependent businesses operating adjacent to the bulkhead (U.S. Department of Commerce, 1992).

Intergovernmental Relationships

There are myriad agencies, departments, organizations, divisions, and every other form of bureaucracy with regulatory authority over the coastal zone. Federal, state, regional, and local governments all have some degree of control over the natural resources and land uses within their respective jurisdictions. How these various levels of government coordinate or fail to coordinate their activities can have pronounced impact on the effectiveness of coastal zone management. All levels of government have an interest in effective management of coastal lands, and should have the opportunity to support their particular positions when deciding how coastal lands will be used. Since land use decisions are necessarily local in nature, many argue that increased responsibility should be placed on the local government and citizenry. However, many land and natural resource use decisions are of greater-than-local impact. Therefore, state, regional, and federal regulatory control should also be in place to ensure that the rights and interests of all populations are protected.

Federal-state concurrent jurisdiction in coastal management has increased in recent years, and there is more sharing of power in the same geographic area (Finnell, 1985). Grant-in-aid programs, CZMA in particular, have provided incentives for state and local governments to implement coastal land management programs, with the federal government providing financial and technical assistance and setting some national standards. Likewise, many state coastal management programs encourage or mandate local coastal governments to create land use plans and regulations.

Despite the growing power exercised by state and local governments in regulating the coastal zone, the federal government has not abdicated all power in this region. The Commerce Clause of the U.S. Constitution has provided the federal government wide-ranging authority to enact economic, environmental, and social regulatory programs. In effect, there exists a federal police power over critical coastal resources. The expansive sweep of the commerce power allows the national government to regulate external effects in major watersheds, wetlands, and beaches if Congress so desires. Furthermore, under the Supremacy Clause of the U.S. Constitution, irreconcilable conflicts between national and state regulation are resolved in favor of the national government (Finnell, 1985).

Congress not only has direct regulatory control over coastal resources, but through other means it also controls the coast and how others can use it. The federal government is the largest single spender in the nation, and the manner in which federal dollars are allocated has a profound impact on federal and state relationships. Significant national policies have been promulgated by Congress through expenditure of tax dollars.

The California coastal management program is an example of state and local governmental power sharing. To a large degree, land use decisions are left to the discretion of local governments, with considerable oversight and control by the state when sensitive coastal resources are involved.

California's 1976 Coastal Act contains several features which promote local involvement and responsibility in coastal management while ensuring that state and regional concerns will not be abdicated.

For instance, development decisions made by a local government in the context of a state-approved coastal program are in most instances considered final. However, certain projects and activities in sensitive resource areas are subject to appeal to the state commission (Finnell, 1985).

The California coastal management program also recognizes the need for horizontal as well as lateral coordination among government actions. The 1976 California Coastal Act mandates a certain degree of coordination between the coastal program and other state functions. The Act recognizes that the geographic and substantive jurisdiction of coastal decision-makers should not be divorced from related housing, transportation, energy, and other issues of concern to all the state's inhabitants (Finnell, 1985).

Florida is another state with a coastal management program that attempts to integrate government decision-making at all levels. Florida has been labeled a "land-use laboratory" (T. Pelham, cited in Finnell, 1985), having "experimented" with a wide range of management models for allocating land and water regulatory power between state and local governments. For instance, Florida's coastal program has included such elements as state establishment of criteria and standards for local implementation, subject to administrative review and enforcement for compliance; direct state land and water use planning and regulation; or state administrative review for consistency with the management program of all development plans, projects, or land and water use regulations proposed by any state or local authority or private developer (Finnell, 1985).

Florida's planning framework can be visualized as a pyramid of government action. Planning at the base is done primarily by local governments pursuant to the Local Government Comprehensive Planning Act of 1975; at the mid-level by regional agencies, such as regional councils of government under the Florida State and Regional Planning Act of 1984, which address problems and plan solutions that are of greater-than-local concern or scope; and at the vortex by state agencies, such as the Executive Office of the Governor and the state land-planning agency (Finnell, 1985).

Although the Florida program allows greater discretion to local governments in coastal management decision-making, the process is not without its drawbacks. While the state approves coastal elements of local plans, it apparently does not do much to ensure that localities carry out the written intentions for resource management. Enforcement is one weak link in the Florida management chain, although it is certainly not an isolated problem among all the coastal states that are grappling with the issue of intergovernmental relationships.

Areas of Particular Concern

Many state coastal management programs give heightened protection to certain especially sensitive areas of their coastal zones. Coastal programs may define Areas of Particular Concern and impose more stringent development or permit requirements in these designated areas. Often Areas of Particular Concern are geographically defined; other states may designate these areas according to the natural resources or habitats present or according to the function performed by a particular coastal feature.

In North Carolina, a major aspect of the regulatory system established by the Coastal Area Management Act (CAMA) involves the designation of Areas of Environmental Concern (AEC) by the North Carolina Coastal Resources Council (CRC). There are 13 categories of AEC, all of which are identified as areas in which uncontrolled or incompatible development might result in irreversible damage. The 13 AEC categories are separated into four broad groupings: estuarine system areas, coastal natural hazard areas, water supply areas, and fragile coastal natural and cultural resource areas. All water areas and about three percent of the land area of the 20 coastal counties in North Carolina are presently designated as AECs.

Permit-letting and enforcement integrate the planning and AEC designation processes. The state shares land use planning powers only in AECs. Local governments retain their traditional regulatory authority in non-AECs, with the exception of statutorily defined "major developments," which must receive approval from the state regardless of local coastal jurisdiction.

Thus, AECs afford a stricter degree of control over development activities in areas of the North Carolina coast where such control is warranted, without reducing the powers of local governments to make their own land use decisions where such local responsibility is appropriate. (For a more detailed discussion of the North Carolina AEC system, see Chapter 7.)

The Florida Environmental Land and Water Management Act of 1972 established Areas of Critical State Concern to protect certain geographic areas so sensitive by their nature and characteristics that development within them would likely have substantial extraterritorial effects (Finnell, 1985). Through the Critical Areas process, the state specifies standards with which land development regulations enacted by the affected local government must comply. The standards apply to the discrete geographic areas designated as Critical Areas by the Governor and the Cabinet. If a local government fails to submit adequate regulations, the state prepares and adopts suitable land use regulations to be administered by local authorities. The designation of Critical Areas is subject to legislative review, and land development regulations adopted within Critical Areas are effective only upon such review. The local government is responsible for issuing projects in Critical Areas. The local government's decision to issue or deny the permit is final, unless appealed to the Florida Land and Water Adjudicatory Commission (Finnell, 1985).

Ocean Management

In recent years there has been increasing concern on the part of both coastal managers and the citizenry at large about activities occurring offshore and the potential impacts on sensitive marine ecosystems. State coastal programs have historically concerned themselves with managing land use activities occurring in and around the coastal shoreline. A number of states are now moving in the direction of expanding the geographical and ecological scope of their management programs, taking into account extensive offshore marine habitats. This expansion takes them more squarely into the areas of fisheries, marine mammals, unique marine habitats (e.g., offshore reefs), as well as proposals for oil and gas development and mineral extraction.

The state of Oregon is the first to have developed a full-fledged ocean management plan, while a number of states are currently pursuing the Oregon model and developing their own programs (e.g., see Hout, 1990; Lowry, 1990; Christie and Johnson, 1990; for an early review of state programs and capabilities in this area, see King and Olsen, 1990). The Oregon legislature enacted its Ocean Resources Management Act in 1987 (SB630), initiating an ocean planning process and creating a 21-member Ocean Resources Management Task Force.

The Task Force oversees the development of the Oregon Resources Management Plan. This plan resulted in extensive analyses of ocean uses, resources, and conditions, and is intended to provide an overall management framework to guide activities and decisions within the 200-mile EEZ (a more detailed Territorial Sea Management Plan has also been prepared). The Oregon program has broken new ground in a number of respects, for instance, by proposing the establishment of an Ocean Stewardship Area, which would extend to the seaward edge of the continental shelf (with a width varying from 35 to 80 miles), and in which management activities would be focused. The Oregon program eventually envisions a system of federal-state co-management of ocean resources and the establishment of new coordinating mechanisms for bringing this about, such as the establishment of an Ocean Policy Advisory Council (e.g., see Hout, 1990).

The challenge for such initiatives in ocean planning is to overcome the differences in jurisdictional points of view about how these areas should be managed. For instance, recent federal administrations have been inclined to support offshore oil and gas development, frequently in direct conflict with state officials and citizens. Indeed, much of the impetus behind programs like Oregon's comes from such federal proposals for oil and gas development.

The Success of CZMA

There are several different ways in which the success and effectiveness of the CZMA might be evaluated. Participation is one measure of success, providing an indicator of the extent to which the financial and other incentives are effective inducements. Based on participation rates, the program has been quite successful. Of the 35 coastal states and territories eligible for funding, 29 now have federally approved plans (notable holdouts have been Texas and Georgia, with each now moving toward developing an approvable program).

Another perhaps more relevant gauge of success is the extent to which state and local management capacity has actually increased in response to CZMA. There is little doubt that CZMA has served as a catalyst for the development of more extensive and more effective coastal management programs. Compared with the state management framework existing prior to CZMA, it is clear that coastal development patterns and practices are more respectful of protecting coastal resources and reducing exposure of people and property to coastal risks. As Godschalk and Cousins (1985) conclude: "When the plans, policies, regulations, and personnel of these individual programs are added up, the result is a quantum leap over 1972 institutional capacity for coastal planning and management."

The CZMA has not been without its problems and limitations, however. One concern stems from the very flexibility of the program, heralded by many as a virtue. While state programs must include certain basic provisions and address certain issues, coastal states need not adopt very stringent or aggressive coastal management requirements. While states like North Carolina have adopted fairly extensive erosion-based setback requirements, other states enforce no shoreline setback at all. Some coastal states have adopted aggressive wetland protection and habitat acquisition programs, while other states have taken no actions in these areas. CZMA, then, has failed to include clear performance standards and to impose on states a clear minimum level of coastal management stringency. It is generally up to each coastal state to determine the extent to which it desires to stringently manage coastal resources. Some states such as South Carolina have even been able to severely curtail their management programs with no federal repercussions at all. Despite CZMA's strong statement of goals and findings, the program has had difficulty articulating clear substantive standards of state performance. This has, understandably, made NOAA's (OCRM) efforts to evaluate state program performance and compliance, required under CZMA, difficult.

In response to this perceived limitation, some have argued the need for clear substantive standards of review and a stronger system for monitoring and evaluating state program compliance. Concerning the first issue, perhaps certain minimum standards of shoreline management or hazard area management ought to be stipulated (e.g., a mandatory erosion-based setback).

Conclusions

The U.S. approach to coastal management has been one of collaboration and partnership between the federal government and state governments. Under the CZMA, Congress created positive incentives (e.g., financial, consistency) for states to develop and implement coastal management programs. Most states have taken advantage of these opportunities, and the CZMA appears to have been a major catalyst for expanded state coastal management. Prior to CZMA many states had little or no coastal management or planning capability.

While state coastal programs must meet certain minimum criteria, CZMA has provided states with considerable flexibility in devising programs which meet their own unique physical and political circumstances. Certain common components of state programs have been identified and discussed, including local planning requirements; shoreline management and retreat provisions (e.g., shoreline setbacks); restrictions to shore-hardening structures; coastal wetlands restrictions; provisions to guide and manage reconstruction; beach access and land acquisition; building codes and construction standards; and ocean management. While the stringency of coastal management varies substantially from state to state, substantial progress has been made since the 1970s in ensuring safer and less destructive coastal development patterns.

7

Regional Planning and Ecosystem Managment

Introduction

Natural resource management does not lend itself to traditional planning and management mechanisms. Indeed, while these fragile resources are often those in need of the greatest protection from the impacts of development, the defined coastal region can be particularly elusive when regulatory regimes attempt to provide the requisite buffer from human encroachment. One reason for this difficulty in managing coastal resources is that all natural resources are included within a system of interacting components, physical and biological, and one action, whether initiated from within or external to the system, will have ramifications far beyond the initial impact. Another major reason for the difficulty in managing coastal resource uses is the fact that natural resources often transcend political boundaries and do not conform to our artificial and arbitrary regulatory and administrative jurisdictions.

One solution that has been posed to address this dilemma is management of natural resources at the *regional* level. Together with a similar approach to natural resource management, the ecosystem approach, regionalism has proven in some cases to have the potential to be the most effective means of ensuring the continued viability of our coastal areas.

Jurisdictional Problems Addressed by Regional Planning

Environmental statutes and regulations are promulgated at both the federal and state levels. In addition, local governments may also pass ordinances which address environmental concerns. This combination of authorities and institutions can often lead to confusion when conflicting policies and duplicative or inconsistent permit requirements exist. Furthermore, some regional environmental problems may not be addressed at all. Federal and state programs may be too broad in scope to deal with an area's particular concerns, while local government solutions may only be able to solve a portion of the problem. The following paragraphs describe some of the drawbacks that might become apparent, and which regional management attempts to address, when each of the traditional levels of government attempt to regulate natural resources.

Federal Policy

The first such drawback involves federal policy, which is often too broad to adequately protect the environmental resources of certain areas. Statutes such as the Clean Water Act and the National Environmental Policy Act must necessarily establish broad goals and standards applicable nationwide. Smaller areas on the regional scale, however, frequently require specific environmental management strategies regulating activities such as land development and pollution discharge in order to preserve their sensitive natural systems. The site-specific environmental necessities of certain areas are often not addressed in federal legislation.

Furthermore, federal environmental policies are not designed to mitigate multi-jurisdictional conflicts or address regional issues. Managing wide areas requires cooperation among all levels of government. Although federal policies can mandate state and local compliance with environmental standards, they often do not establish a basis for intergovernmental cooperation. Most federal policies do not mitigate conflicts between municipal, county, and state governments regarding authority over and responsibility for management planning. Rather, these policies frequently act as enforcement agents by concentrating more on delegating responsibility to the states than on working collectively to address regional issues.

State Policy

While states are given much authority to carry out federal mandates and programs of their own, there are often problems associated with natural resource management at the state level. State environmental agencies are usually the parties responsible for environmental quality within the state. State agencies may be subject to broad federal standards; but it is the states, not the federal government, which are responsible for creating implementation plans and drafting regulations.

For a number of reasons, however, state agencies may fail to discern and address the needs of certain environmentally sensitive areas. For instance, existing programs and regulations may be too broad in scope. As with federal environmental statutes and regulations, state standards are intended to address large areas and therefore are not tailored to meet the needs of particularly sensitive areas.

Local Policy

Although state agencies administer most environmental regulations, local governments play an important role in natural resource protection. Many state regulations are implemented and enforced at the local level. Through the police-power and state-enabling legislation, local governments are responsible for land use planning, zoning, and subdivision regulations. There are, however, several limitations to natural resource protection at the local level.

One such limitation lies in the fact that natural ecosystems transcend local boundaries. Local political borders do not correspond to natural ecosystems, and natural resource management plans are often developed around jurisdictional boundaries without fully incorporating the natural systems that are to be protected. This problem is especially true if land use management is required to protect resources, as the regulation of land use is a local domain. For example, through their land use practices, all localities within a watershed affect the water quality for all users of that watershed. Uncoordinated efforts to improve water quality by individual localities through land use regulations may be hindered as a result of activities in other jurisdictions, whose land use laws may not be as stringent.

In addition, local governance is largely fragmented among numerous counties and municipalities. Activities or problems in one jurisdiction, such as nonpoint source pollution, may affect other localities. Traditionally there is a lack of framework for dealing with regional issues or problems and there are generally no incentives for protecting resources of regional significance.

Within localities, authority may be fragmented among various agencies, special districts, or service districts. For example, programs and regulations affecting the environment, planning, housing, and infrastructure may be carried out by independent agencies. As a result, the local permit process is also fragmented, and there is generally no coordination between local and state or federal permit processes.

A final drawback is that local governments may have provincial or parochial outlooks. The regulation of land and natural resources is a political decision, and local decisions tend to reflect local political influences which often do not take into account greater-than-local concerns. All too often there is no reason for localities to consider impacts beyond their border or outside of their extraterritorial jurisdiction. Economic development and the pressure to create jobs and increase the tax base may take precedence over other wider community goals. As a result, some local governments may be prodevelopment at any cost, although competition for economic development among localities can substantially reduce any benefits. An urban and rural dichotomy may be a problem as well, as rural residents may resent conservation efforts that are seen as deterring growth.

Ecosystem Management

A planning and management concept closely related to regionalism which attempts to reach similar goals in natural resource management is the ecosystem approach. This involves the concept of interaction among environmental factors, living organisms, and human beings in a holistic, sustainable system, usually referred to as an ecosystem. (National Research Council of the U.S., 1985).

The ecosystem approach is based on the premise that land, water, air, and biota interact and are mutually influenced. Existing resource management approaches which partition the environment into separate components of land, water, and air with associated biota are recognized as inadequate from the ecosystem perspective, "since management of a resource component in isolation from adjacent or interacting components would likely produce short-sighted strategies to protect one component of the environment at the expense of another" (Caldwell, 1985).

The ecosystem approach often involves issues of intergenerational equity. As resources are exploited, whether directly or as a depository for wastes, we also affect the use that future generations will be able to make of that resource. The present generation has the ability in some instances to magnify the benefits of certain resources for future generations, for example, by implementing navigational aids along a waterway. Other actions of the current population, however, will decrease the utility of certain resources, or severely increase the cost of its use for future generations, as in the case of the dumping of toxic wastes. Future generations are generally unrepresented when policy decisions regarding the use of a natural resource are made, and so the present generation, however unwittingly, often lessens the flexibility that the future generation will have in using that resource (National Research Council of U.S., 1985).

The ecosystem approach to natural resource management has the potential to embody the principles of intergenerational equity. One such principle is that there should be a concerted effort toward conservation of quality of the resource, which entails leaving the ecosystem in no worse condition than it was received from previous generations. The second such principle for intergenerational equity involves conserving the diversity of the natural resource base, so that future generations have as many options regarding its use as are present today.

There are many different approaches to implementing regional or ecosystem management. In some areas, management is undertaken by a regulatory agency. This may take the form of a free-standing body spanning state borders, or it may operate within a state government, either as a separate entity or as a division of an existing state department or agency. Such regulatory agencies are usually created by the legislators of the state(s) and may be given both regulatory and enforcement powers. Other regional management bodies are more administrative in nature and may perform coordinating functions or act as advisory boards to state and/or local governments.

Many states have legislation which enables localities to voluntarily form Councils of Government (COGs). For instance, in North Carolina, legislation allows COGs to be created to study and inventory regional roles, resources, and problems, and promote cooperative arrangements and coordinated action among their member governments. Planning districts can also be formed for the basis of COGs, where participating governments pay dues to the COG and each locality sends a delegate to COG planning meetings. COGs are similar in nature to regional planning commissions, which are often formed to prepare regional plans to address land uses, public works, and economic development strategies.

The following sections discuss several manifestations of the regional or ecosystem approach to natural resource management. To a greater or lesser degree, each of these programs attempts to deal with the problems of multiple jurisdictions and to cross political borders in order to manage natural systems by following natural boundaries.

The National Estuary Program

The National Estuary Program (NEP) was established in 1987 by the Federal Water Pollution Control Act, and is administered by the U.S. Environmental Protection Agency (EPA) through the Office of Wetlands, Oceans and Watersheds (OWOW). The Act defines the NEP's primary goals to be the protection and improvement of water quality and the enhancement of living resources (33 U.S.C.S. §1330(a)(2)(A)). Before this formal declaration, however, the roots of the NEP had already been established through efforts to manage the coastal environment at both the federal and state levels. In particular, the EPA's involvement in the Great Lakes Program and the Chesapeake Bay Program supported the basic premise of the NEP: that management of hydrologic ecosystems must be approached holistically by recognizing the interconnections of all living resources within the estuarine environment. The NEP also relies on past experience, which demonstrates that a regional, cooperative approach to natural resources protection and management is both feasible and effective.

The National Estuary Program is a voluntary program operated at the state level. Federal technical and financial assistance is available to the states in order to identify an estuary's problems and to develop a management plan of action to address those problems. The management approach used by each program follows federal standards which are flexible enough to allow for considerable local variation in problem selection and managerial design. While federal planning funds are provided through the NEP, state and local governments are responsible for funding implementation of the management plan.

The NEP encompasses estuaries which represent diverse ecosystems, including both heavily urbanized and rural watersheds, each of which has its own attending ecological, social, and economic issues to be addressed. Furthermore, some of the estuaries of the NEP transcend both local and state boundaries, and many differ in their degree of jurisdictional complexity. To deal with these differences among estuaries, the structure of each individual NEP centers around its own Management Conference, comprised of various committees which oversee the various program activities undertaken by that particular NEP. The Conference also acts as the primary decision-making unit. There is considerable variation in the composition and size of the individual Management Conferences, depending upon the specific conditions of each estuary program.

While the EPA allows for flexibility in composition, each Management Conference must contain several committees, headed by a policy committee, made up of EPA representatives, governor(s), and top agency officials. The Conference also includes a management committee, which acts as the consensus builder for the group as a whole and whose members are representatives of state water quality and natural resource agencies, state regulatory offices, and community and environmental groups. The management committee is responsible for developing the five-year Management Conference Agreement between the state and EPA, which identifies program activities, work products, and sets major program milestones and work schedules. Other committees found in a Management Conference include a science and technical advisory committee, a citizens' advisory committee, a local government committee, and a financial planning committee.

The various committees of each NEP Management Conference work together to achieve seven basic federally mandated purposes, with the underlying understanding that the ultimate goal of the NEP is to achieve basinwide planning to control pollution and manage living resources. The seven legislatively determined purposes of a Management Conference are

- assess trends in water quality, natural resources, and estuary uses

- data collection and assessment of toxins, nutrients, and natural resources within the estuarine zone in order to identify the causes of environmental problems

- develop the relationship between the point and nonpoint loadings of pollutants to the estuarine zone and the potential uses of the zone, water quality, and natural resources

- develop a Comprehensive Conservation and Management Plan (CCMP) that includes recommendations for priority corrective actions and compliance schedules addressing sources of pollution and restoration of the biological, chemical, and physical integrity of the estuarine zone

- develop plans for the coordinated implementation of the CCMP by states as well as the federal and local agencies participating in the Conference

- monitor the effectiveness of actions taken pursuant to the plan

- review federal financial assistance programs and federal development programs for consistency with the CCMP (33 U.S.C.S. §1330(b)).

The Comprehensive Conservation and Management Plans are the heart of each NEP, but their implementability remains questionable. While federal assistance covers preparation and planning, no federal monies are available for implementation. Therefore, responsibility for putting the plans into action rests entirely with state and participating local governments. Furthermore, while the CCMP operates as a vehicle for problem identification, the plans do not automatically become state public policy. Further political action, along with budgetary and public support, is often required before a CCMP gets on the state agenda. Despite the limitations in terms of policy execution and implementation financing, the structure of the National Estuary Program may prove to be flexible and adaptable enough to be successful in managing estuaries of national significance (Imperial et al., 1993).

Special Area Management Planning

Special Area Management Planning (SAMP) is a coordinated approach which addresses complex and often far-reaching environmental problems through regional management. The Federal Coastal Zone Management Act defines a special area management plan as a "comprehensive plan providing for natural resource protection and reasonable coastal-dependent economic growth containing a detailed and comprehensive statement of policies; standards and criteria to guide public and private uses of lands and waters; and mechanisms for timely implementation in specific geographic areas within the coastal zone" (16 U.S.C. §1453(17)).

As a planning mechanism, special area management has been used with varying degrees of success throughout the United States. While specific applications of SAMP vary widely, the basic tenets of the technique are designed to accomplish similar broad goals, including

- address environmental problems that are best solved through a multi-jurisdictional and integrated policy approach

- coordinate existing policies in order to adequately and comprehensively address environmental problems

- establish a balanced management framework for the protection of public or socially important resources, while allowing for appropriate continued use of these resources.

There are several scenarios in which SAMP may be appropriate. First, environmental problems that warrant this approach typically involve natural systems lying within multiple political jurisdictions. Conflicts regarding the multiple use of resources, including numerous human and natural forces which may threaten the vitality of the resource, may make management by a single entity problematic. Second, high resource values (economic, recreational, social, biological) often create conflicting interests regarding preservation or development, and in these cases an integrated special area approach allows for more flexible, tailored management. A publicly or socially important natural resource area (characterized as a "public good") may also be targeted for special area management. Finally, particularly severe environmental problems ranging over a large geographic area may warrant the use of this management technique.

Special area management is founded upon specific management goals and objectives pertaining to an explicit, well-defined problem area. Typically, this area is delineated spatially, according to resource-area boundaries which include the environmental system targeted by management goals and the human systems that impact upon it.

Natural, political, and social systems within this area must also be identified. The planning area must also encompass a broad enough area to include the entire relevant environmental system in addition to the human systems that impact upon it.

In its best form, special area management plan participants typically work together through consensus and negotiation to create an agreed-upon management text. Various interest groups can be involved in the SAMP process, including state and federal agencies, local officials, environmentalists, landowners, developers, citizen groups, and others with a stake in the management of a particular area.

The final outcome of the special area management process can take several forms. Some SAMPs end as a loose nonenforceable coalition of interests who confer with one another concerning policy goals. Other plans operate by means of an advisory committee which counsels relevant governmental units on how to deal with specific problems. Still other SAMPs become a formal part of either state or local government and are often given some degree of regulatory control.

Special areas can range in size from a relatively small tract, such as San Bruno Mountain's 3,400 acres, to a massive area, such as the Adirondack State Park, which encompasses six million acres in rural upstate New York. Although these two areas may initially appear to have nothing in common, both contain valuable natural resources that are subject to a complex web of competing interests, and which the SAMP technique helps to protect and preserve.

A prime example of a SAMP in the United States is the Chesapeake Bay Program. The Chesapeake Bay is the largest estuary in the United States, being 195 miles long and from 4 to 30 miles wide. Approximately 50 major rivers and over 100 smaller tributaries provide freshwater to the bay. The drainage basin includes an area of roughly 64,000 square miles, thus accounting for one-sixth of the Atlantic seaboard.

Responding to public concern regarding the declining water quality and the diminishing fish and shellfish landings, in 1975 EPA conducted a comprehensive study of the Chesapeake Bay. The findings of the five-year study prompted the governors of the states of Maryland, Virginia, Pennsylvania, the mayor of the District of Columbia, the chairman of the Chesapeake Bay Commission, and the administrator of the EPA to sign the 1983 Chesapeake Bay Agreement (CBA). Of the states within the watershed, only Delaware, New York, and West

Virginia have not signed the CBA, though the 1992 amendments state that members should "explore cooperative working relationships" with these states.

The Chesapeake Bay Agreement relies entirely upon individual state implementation of the goal and policy statements. Thus each state has approached watershed management differently. This has allowed flexibility in developing a management program that is politically acceptable to each state. In addition, the setting of priorities, goals, and objectives are established by consensus.

The Great Lakes Program

The Great Lakes are the most important natural resource shared by Canada and the United States. The joint responsibility for this shared resource has produced large-scale cooperative arrangements such as the St. Lawrence Seaway, the Niagara Falls Treaty, the Great Lakes Water Quality Agreements, the Great Lakes Fishery Commission, and three Lake Levels Boards of Control. The institutional setting within which these management activities occur is complex and diverse. The responsibility for governance is diffused among the two federal governments, eight American states, the province of Ontario, as well as among numerous regional, local, and special purpose districts of government.

With relatively few exceptions, the lakes themselves are not directly managed. There are, of course, specific instances of direct management—such as the regulation of water levels or the manipulation of biota (for example, species of fish). But the major task of environmental protection for the lakes involves managing certain activities of people. The greater body of law and policy is directed toward those human activities that affect the lakes and their quality (Caldwell, 1985). This section describes one such management system, the Great Lakes Program (GLP), which began in the early 1970s as a cooperative effort between the United States and Canada to address the environmental problems facing the Great Lakes ecosystem.

The GLP is a true inter-jurisdictional effort which encompasses the entire watershed of the Great Lakes. The United States and Canada base their respective management programs on a series of international agreements, the Great Lakes Water Quality Agreements (GLWQA) (Imperial et al., 1993). The first GLWQA was signed in Ottawa by President Nixon and Prime Minister Trudeau. Following the first five-year review, the GLWQA of 1978 was signed at Ottawa.

The International Joint Commission (IJC) plays an important role in guiding the efforts of the two countries and monitoring the progress of implementation of the GLP. The IJC has a history pre-dating the GLWQA, and was actually established in 1909 by the Boundary Waters Treaty between the United States and Canada to oversee navigation, water withdrawl, and water levels. Today the IJC is the most prominent public body shaping policy with respect to the Great Lakes, and it is a testament to the Commission's effectiveness in that it continues to oversee management today. The U.S. portion of the GLP is administered by the Great Lakes National Program Office (GLNPO), which is a separate and distinct office within the U.S. Environmental Protection Agency.

With careful study of biannual and five-year progress reports, the Great Lakes Program has been able to evolve over the years to deal with increasingly complex issues involving the integrity of the Great Lakes environment. As scientific data is acquired and interpreted, and as new understandings of the ecosystem have been reached, the GLP has been able to update and adapt its management programs to respond to the lakes' environmental needs.

The first GLWQA, signed in 1972, contained general objectives and addressed conventional pollutants. The early years of the program focused primarily on point sources of pollution in order to address the problems of oxygen depletion and eutrophication. To achieve these goals, major municipal treatment plants within the management area were required to reduce phosphorus in effluents, and phosphate detergents were banned in many states (Imperial et al., 1993).

The 1978 Agreement added more specific and quantitative objectives, including physical, microbiological, and radiological parameters (Imperial et al., 1993). Specific objectives of the Agreement include a nondegradation clause, a policy that flow augmentation is not a substitute for adequate treatment, exclusion of inshore areas where natural phenomena prevent achievement of objectives, and designation of limited-use zones.

The 1978 GLWQA is most notable for being the first major international treaty or agreement to embrace the ecosystem approach to the management of large regional resources (National Research Council of U.S., 1985). Thus, by formal agreement between Canada and the United States, policies directed toward the restoration and enhancement of water quality in the Great Lakes were to be based upon a basinwide ecosystem view (Caldwell, 1985).

The 1978 GLWQA took a long-term perspective in managing pollutant threats, recognizing the need for both reactive and preventive measures to control the buildup of substances and the transport of materials from the land to the water and from the air to the water. In the Agreement, the water resources of the basin transcend political boundaries within the basin and are treated as a single hydrologic system (National Research Council of the U.S., 1985).

Article I(g) of the 1978 GLWQA defines the Great Lakes ecosystem as "the interacting components of air, land, water and living organisms, including man" (Caldwell, 1985). This ecosystem approach means that actions affecting the lakes, taken or authorized by the governments, must "proceed on the understanding that the field of policy is no less than the basinwide watershed of the Great Lakes and the multifarious relationships interacting within and intruding from without" (Caldwell, 1985).

The Great Lakes Program has evolved substantially since the 1972 GLWQA. The adoption of a basinwide ecosystem approach to management for the lakes is a decision of major international importance (Caldwell, 1985). Aside from this more general achievement, progress in specific areas has also been notable. For instance, phosphorous loadings from point sources have been reduced by an estimated 80–90% through regulation and financial assistance; all major dischargers as a group are currently meeting the 1 mg/liter phosphorous goal; the GLP is now targeting the control of nonpoint sources of nutrients; support is being given to efforts to obtain information about sources, fates, and effects of pollutants to support a mass balance approach in remedial action programs; point-source loadings of almost all toxic substances have decreased in recent years; and the GLP is working to assess and address the problem of contaminated bottom sediments (Imperial et al., 1993).

There are also some lessons to be learned from the Great Lakes Program that can be applied to other ecosystem-based management approaches. For instance, without clearly articulated goals and priorities to drive the decisions and actions of the GLP, its efforts have frequently lacked focus. This problem is exacerbated in a management system that is highly complex and involves many levels of government. Furthermore, it is clear that it is crucial to set risk-based goals and priorities and let the priorities drive the management decisions and actions. The GLP will never have the authority or the resources to address all of the problems in the Great Lakes, and it is important that these resources be flexibly targeted and integrated in a manner that provides the greatest opportunity from the limited availability of resources (Imperial et al., 1993).

North Carolina Areas of Environmental Concern

The North Carolina Coastal Area Management Act (CAMA) protects natural resources in the coastal zone through an ecosystem approach by designating certain geographic areas as Areas of Environmental Concern (AECs). The 13 categories of AEC designated as such by the North Carolina Coastal Resources Commission (CRC) include water as well as land, and are identified as areas in which uncontrolled or incompatible development might result in irreversible damage. CAMA further instructs the CRC to determine what types of development activities are appropriate within such areas, and it calls on local government to give special attention to these environmentally fragile and important areas when developing land use plans. Also, CAMA provided that upon establishing the types of development activities appropriate within AECs, the CRC would implement a permit program capable of controlling any inappropriate or damaging development activities within the AECs. The intent of this authority is not to stop development but rather to ensure the compatibility of development with the continued productivity and value of certain critical land and water areas (15A NCAC 7H .0102(e)).

The Act divides the implementation responsibilities of the permit program between local governments and the Coastal Resources Commission. Individuals proposing "minor development" activities within an AEC are required to receive permits from a local permit officer, while individuals undertaking "major development" activities must seek permits directly from the CRC.

As presented in the guidelines accompanying CAMA, the 13 categories of AECs are separated into four broad groupings. The broad breakdowns include categories of AECs that are either interrelated components of an ecological system or a collection of AECs with similar management objectives. The purpose in presenting the material in this manner is not only to create a logical organization, but also to emphasize the relationship of one AEC category to another and the interactive nature of AECs within the total coastal environment (15A NCAC 7H .0103(b)).

The first AECs discussed collectively in the CAMA regulations are those within the estuarine system, and include the following AEC categories: estuarine waters, coastal wetlands, public trust areas, and estuarine shorelines. The next broad grouping is composed of those AECs that are considered natural hazard areas along the Atlantic shoreline. Ocean hazard areas include beaches, frontal dunes, inlet lands, and other areas with the possibility of erosion or flood damage.

The third broad grouping of AECs includes valuable small surface water supply watersheds and public water supply wellfields. The fourth and final group of AECs is gathered under the heading of fragile coastal natural and cultural resource areas, and is defined as areas containing "environmental, natural or cultural resources of more than local significance in which uncontrolled or incompatible development could result in major or irreversible damage to natural systems or cultural resources, scientific, educational, or associative values, or aesthetic qualities" (15A NCAC 7H .0501). The AECs within this grouping include coastal complex natural areas, coastal areas that sustain remnant species, unique coastal geologic formations, and significant coastal architectural resources.

The state guidelines provide detailed descriptions of each Area of Environmental Concern, explain the significance of the areas, outline management objectives, and set forth use standards for each type of AEC.

The designation of AECs, the development of use standards adopted by the CRC, and the implementation of the permit process in conformance with these standards are an application of ecosystem management within the context of the North Carolina Coastal Management Program. The Coastal Resources Commission has reserved AEC designation for areas of particular importance or vulnerability; not all coastal resource areas become CAMA Areas of Environmental Concern.

The Watershed Protection Approach

All states and the federal government have water protection programs designed to reverse or prevent water quality degradation. Most of these programs include regulations on industrial and municipal point source discharges. One of the greatest dangers to the nation's water supply, however, emanates from nonpoint sources of pollution, such as runoff into waterways and seepage into groundwaters. Wetland degradation and habitat destruction are also threatened by these nonpoint sources of pollution.

There are now in place some federal programs aimed at nonpoint source pollution. However, absolute uniform regulation of nonpoint sources at the federal level would be prohibitively expensive. Furthermore, such federally imposed control would most likely be politically infeasible in our federalist system, where impingements on traditional state and local prerogatives such as land use regulation and economic development are not frequently tolerated. Because of these limitations on any federal system of regulation, governments at all levels are broadening their outlook on water quality protection and refocusing existing water pollution control programs to operate in a more comprehensive and coordinated manner. There is a growing consensus that the pollution and habitat degradation problems now facing society can best be solved by following a basinwide approach that takes into account the dynamic relationships that sustain natural resources and their beneficial uses. The term "watershed protection approach" is often used to encompass these ideas (U.S. Environmental Protection Agency, 1991).

The term "watershed," as used in the United States, refers to a geographic area in which water, sediments, and dissolved materials drain to a common outlet—a point on a larger stream, a lake, an underlying aquifer, an estuary, or an ocean. This area is also called the "drainage basin" of the receiving water body.

When defining the boundaries of the watershed in a particular locality for purposes of regulation, many factors may be considered. Local decisions on the scale of geographic unit may involve analysis of the hydrologic aspects of underlying groundwaters, economic uses, the type and scope of pollution problems, and the level of resources available for protection and restoration projects (U.S. Environmental Protection Agency, 1991).

The watershed protection approach aims at targeted, cooperative, and integrated action. Three main principles are usually relied upon. First, the target watersheds should be those where pollution poses the greatest risk to human health, ecological resources, desirable uses of the water, or a combination of these. This risk-based geographic targeting may involve several different problems that pose health or ecological risks in the watershed. These problems include industrial wastewater discharges; municipal wastewater, stormwater, and combined sewer overflows; waste dumping and injection; nonpoint source runoff or seepage; accidental leaks and spills of toxic or hazardous substances; atmospheric deposition; habitat alteration, including wetlands loss; and flow variations. Based on evaluation of these and similar problems, the highest-risk watersheds are identified and one or more are selected for cooperative, integrated assessment and protection.

The second principle of the watershed protection approach entails stakeholder involvement; all parties with a stake in the specific local situation should participate in the analysis of problems and the creation of solutions. Potential participants in watershed protection projects include state environmental, public health, agricultural, and natural resources agencies; local/regional boards, commissions, and agencies; EPA water and other programs; other federal agencies; Native American tribes; public representatives; private wildlife and conservation organizations; industry sector representatives; and the academic community. Stakeholders should work as a task force, reaching consensus on goals and approaches for addressing a watershed's problems, the specific actions to be taken, and how they will be coordinated and evaluated.

The third principle in the watershed protection approach is that the actions undertaken should draw on the full range of methods and tools available, integrating them into a coordinated, multi-organization attack on the problems. Coordinated action may be taken in such areas as voluntary source reduction programs (e.g., waste minimization, BMPs); permit issuance and enforcement programs, standard setting and enforcement programs (nonpermitting); direct financing; economic incentives; education and information dissemination; technical assistance; remediation of contaminated soil or water; and emergency response to accidental leaks or spills. The selected tools are then applied to the watershed's problems, according to the plans and roles established through stakeholder consensus. Progress is evaluated periodically via ecological indicators and other measures (U.S. Environmental Protection Agency, 1991).

Numerous projects using the watershed protection approach have been implemented throughout the United States, and many more are in various stages of planning. These activities were not mandated by EPA or any other central agency; they have arisen spontaneously as the most effective way to address pressing local or regional problems (U.S. Environmental Protection Agency, 1991). In general, these project differ from conventional water quality initiatives in that they encompass all or most of the landscape in a well-defined watershed or other ecological, physiographic, or hydrologic unit, such as an embayment, an aquifer, or a mountain valley. Most such projects are more comprehensive than traditional water regulations, and establish goals and objectives dealing with a vast array of watershed issues, such as chemical water quality (conventional pollutants and toxics), physical water quality (e.g., temperature, flow, circulation), habitat quality (e.g., channel morphology, composition, and health of biotic communities), and biodiversity (e.g., species number, range) (U.S. Environmental Protection Agency, 1991).

One watershed project which has had some success to date is the Stillaguamish Watershed Protection Project in Washington State. The Stillaguamish Watershed is a significant source of nonpoint source pollution to Puget Sound. Bacteria from livestock wastes and onsite sewage disposal systems are the main pollutants, as well as runoff of sediment from forests, farms, and development sites. In large part because of these pollutants, shellfish beds in Port Susan have been declared unsafe for commercial harvest.

A Watershed Management Committee (WMC) was formed in 1988 with a grant from the Washington Department of Ecology. The WMC was made up of representatives from the Tulalip and Stillaguamish Tribes, county and city governments, environmental and business interests, and homeowners' and citizens' organizations. State and federal environmental regulators participated via a technical advisory committee.

The Stillaguamish Watershed Action Plan, completed in 1989, consists of five source control programs, a public education program, and a monitoring program. WMC recommendations include developing farm conservation plans, reducing improper disposal of human waste, preventing urban runoff, and sampling on a regular basis to track water quality trends (U.S. Environmental Protection Agency, 1991).

Conclusions

This chapter has introduced the regional perspective in coastal management and discussed the primary benefits and advantages of a regional approach. Clearly, many coastal problems, and the coastal ecosystem itself, extend beyond local (and frequently state) jurisdictional boundaries. Regional planning approaches can help to overcome these difficulties. Several key federal and state initiatives have been undertaken and serve to promote regional coastal management. These include the National Estuary Program, Special Area Management Plans (under CZMA), the Great Lakes Program, North Carolina's Areas of Environmental Concern (AECs), and the EPA's Watersheds Protection Program. These and other examples illustrate the potential importance and utility of regional coastal management approaches. Increasingly, regional, ecosystem-oriented strategies will constitute an integral element in effective coastal management in the United States and elsewhere.

8

Local Coastal Managment

Many of the day-to-day planning and management decisions that occur in the coastal zone are made at the local level by hundreds of counties, cities, and towns. In the U.S. management framework, historically local governments have had primary responsibility for managing land use and development. Moreover, it is at the local level, it can be argued, that land use and comprehensive planning can be most responsive to the interests and needs of the constituents and to the special and unique management issues and concerns of the locality.

In this chapter we examine in some detail coastal planning and management at the local level—its potential and existing patterns. As the following discussion will conclude, there is considerable management activity at the local level and many local jurisdictions are implementing creative and effective management programs.

Toward Sustainable Coastal Communities

We believe that coastal localities—located in every state and in every region of the country—have the potential to become sustainable coastal communities. By *sustainable coastal communities* we mean communities (including a variety of local governmental units—counties, cities, towns, villages) that seek to minimize their destructive impact on natural systems and the natural environment, create highly livable and enduring places, and build communities which are socially just and in which the needs of all groups in the community are considered and addressed.

As we have seen earlier, *sustainability* and *sustainable development* have become commonly employed goals of many in the environmental movement and those believing a practical balance between development and conservation is needed. The 1987 report of the Brundtland Commission did much to popularize the concept of sustainable development, defining it as "development that meets the needs of the present without compromising the ability of future generations to meet their own needs."

In more recent years the concept of *sustainable communities* has received increasing attention among urban planners, architects, and others in the design field who see the direct application of these ideas to how cities and towns are designed, planned, and operated.

What more precisely is a sustainable coastal community? While we are hesitant to identify a hard and fast template, or to present a definitive list of characteristics, there are certain features which we believe help to define these localities. A tentative list of these characteristics (adopted from Beatley and Brower, 1993) includes the following:

- Sustainable coastal communities minimize disruption of natural systems and avoid consumption and destruction of ecologically sensitive lands (e.g., coastal wetlands, maritime forests, species habitat, and areas rich in biodiversity)

- Sustainable coastal communities minimize the "human footprint" and reduce the wasteful consumption of land; promote compact, contiguous development patterns and the separation of urban/urbanizable lands from rural/natural lands

- Sustainable coastal communities avoid environmental hazards and reduce the exposure of people and property to coastal hazards by keeping people and property out of coastal floodplains, high-erosion zones, inlet hazard areas, etc.

- Sustainable coastal communities reduce the generation of waste (e.g., air pollution, water pollution) and the consumption of non-renewable resources, and promote the recycling and reuse of waste products; respect the earth's ecological "capital," utilizing and expending only the ecological "interest"; and understand and live within the natural ecological carrying capacities of the area

- Sustainable coastal communities reduce dependence on the automobile and promote a more balanced and integrated transportation system; encourage/facilitate the use of a variety of alternative and more sustainable modes of transportation, including mass transit, bicycles, and walking; and integrate transportation and land use decisions

- Sustainable coastal communities promote and develop a sense of place and an understanding and appreciation of the bioregional context in which they are situated

- Sustainable coastal communities have a high degree of livability; they are aesthetically pleasing and visually stimulating communities, whose architecture, streetscapes, and urban spaces inspire and uplift the human spirit

- Sustainable coastal communities incorporate a strong public and civic dimension, which is reflected in the community's spatial and physical form; they place importance on public spaces and buildings (e.g., squares, pedestrian plazas, courthouses) as locations for social and public interaction, and which help to shape a sense of shared identity

- Sustainable coastal communities promote, whenever possible, a human scale and encourage integration of uses and activities (i.e., commercial, residential) and enhance livability in numerous ways, including reducing trip generation, reducing crime, and providing more active and vibrant urban spaces

- Sustainable coastal communities are communities in which people feel safe—where crime, violence, and threats to life are minimal

- Sustainable coastal communities are communities where residents have opportunities to enjoy a rich and diverse cultural life

- Sustainable coastal communities are socially just communities, which seek to eradicate poverty and ensure a dignified life for all residents; provide affordable housing, health care, meaningful employment, and other basic conditions of a dignified life; reduce the physical and social separation between income and racial groups; and achieve a fair and equitable distribution of environmental and other risks

- Sustainable coastal communities are democratic communities that value the participation of all citizens and provide opportunities for citizens to be actively involved in their governance

The relationship between the concept of sustainable communities and several key functions which local governments are typically involved in is central to coastal zone management. Land use planning is one such activity and involves the allocation and distribution of different allowable uses throughout the community. Certain areas are typically designated for development (e.g., residential, commercial, industrial), while others may be identified as conservation or protected areas. Where some development is allowed, the type density and other characteristics of the development are typically specified. These activities are contained in the community's comprehensive plan (sometimes called the general plan, or master plan), which typically will address a host of other local development issues, including the location of roads, sewer lines, schools, and other public improvements.

In this way, then, land use planning and growth management programs are central to promoting local sustainability and to bringing about sustainable coastal communities. The idea of sustainable communities, however, expands the set of concerns even further. It is concerned not only with how and where land development occurs, but also how the city or community functions once land use decisions are made.

As the discussion below will illustrate, there are few coastal communities that could be described as sustainable communities in the sense that they satisfy all (or even most) of the characteristics we have identified. What is true, however, is that a number of coastal localities are moving in the direction of greater sustainability—communities doing one or more interesting or innovative things that promote increased sustainability.

Overview of Local Coastal Planning and Management

A systematic survey of local coastal programs was conducted by Godschalk et al. (1989), but was aimed at identifying how localities at risk from hurricanes and coastal storms were addressing these hazards. While focused on hurricane and coastal storm mitigation, the survey did reveal patterns of local planning and management.

High-risk coastal localities were asked to indicate, among other things, which planning and management tools they were currently using. Not surprisingly, certain tools and techniques were more commonly utilized than others. These included zoning ordinances, subdivision ordinances, comprehensive plans, and evacuation plans. These management tools were utilized in a larger majority of responding localities and appear quite common (see Table 8.1). More than half of the responding jurisdictions indicated they were implementing a shoreline setback regulation and a capital improvement program. A substantial number of localities also indicated that they were locating public structures and buildings to reduce storm risks, had adopted dune protection regulations, and were locating capital facilities to reduce or discourage development in high-hazard areas.

On the other hand, certain management tools were found not to be in common usage, including impact taxes or special assessments, building relocation programs, acquisition of damaged buildings in hazardous areas, reduced or below-market taxation, and acquisition of development rights or scenic easements.

Responding communities were also asked to evaluate the different management tools in use according to their effectiveness at reducing coastal storm risks. Certain management tools were seen as particularly effective, including special hazard area ordinances, impact taxes or special assessments, dune protection regulations, location of public structures to minimize risk, shoreline setback regulations, and acquisition of undeveloped land in hazard areas (see Table 8.2). Other tools and techniques were viewed as being considerably less effective, including capital improvement programs, acquisition of development rights or scenic easements, and hazard disclosure requirement in real estate transactions.

These findings are encouraging in the sense that they indicate that many coastal localities have adopted some minimum degree of planning and management. These are, albeit, conventional management tools—zoning and subdivision ordinances, comprehensive/land use plans—but they do suggest that most coastal localities have at least begun to manage development and growth. These findings are somewhat more discouraging in that some of the potentially more successful and effective management tools are not as frequently used. These patterns suggest that most coastal localities have not developed very innovative or complex management requirements and have perhaps not

TABLE 8.1

Development Management Measures in Order of Frequency Used[a]

Type of measure	Survey communities using measure	
	Number	Percentage
1. Zoning ordinance	354	87.8
2. Subdivision ordinance	347	86.1
3. Comprehensive/land use plan	340	84.4
4. Evacuation plan	272	67.5
5. Shoreline setback regulation	218	54.1
6. Capital improvement program	216	53.6
7. Location of public structures and buildings to reduce storm risks	185	45.9
8. Dune protection regulations	152	37.7
9. Location of capital facilities to reduce or discourage development in high-hazard areas	126	31.3
10. Acquisition of undeveloped land in hazardous areas	118	29.3
11. Special hazard area ordinance	109	27.0
12. Hazard disclosure requirements in real estate transactions	103	25.6
13. Recovery/reconstruction plan or policies	87	21.6
14. Transfer of development potential from hazardous to nonhazardous sites	84	20.8
15. Hurricane/storm component of comprehensive plan	80	19.9
16. Construction practice seminars	62	15.4
17. Acquisition of development rights or scenic easements	56	13.9
18. Reduced or below-market taxation	44	10.9
19. Acquisition of damaged buildings in hazardous areas	12	3.0
20. Building relocation program	9	2.2
21. Impact taxes or special assessments	7	1.7

Source: Godschalk et al. (1989).

[a]$N = 403$.

discovered certain planning measures that may be highly effective in promoting local sustainability.

What follows is an examination of these different planning and management measures. We will argue that effective local, coastal management programs entail a creative packaging of these different categories of management tools.

TABLE 8.2

Development Management Measures in Order of Perceived Effectiveness[a]

Type of measure	Average effectiveness rating[b]
1. Special hazard area ordinance	3.85
2. Impact taxes or special assessments	3.71
3. Dune protection regulations	3.69
4. Location of public structures to minimize risk	3.67
5. Shoreline setback regulations	3.59
6. Acquisition of undeveloped land in hazard areas	3.58
7. Acquisition of damaged buildings in hazard areas	3.55
8. Evacuation plan	3.53
9. Transfer of development potential from hazardous to nonhazardous sites	3.46
10. Location of capital facilities to reduce or discourage development in high-hazard areas	3.43
11. Hurricane/storm component of comprehensive plan	3.33
12. Building location program	3.33
13. Construction practice seminars	3.24
14. Zoning ordinance	3.16
15. Subdivision ordinance	3.06
16. Reduced or below-market taxation	3.00
17. Recovery/reconstruction plan or policies	2.98
18. Comprehensive/land use plan	2.94
19. Hazard disclosure requirements in real estate transactions	2.93
20. Acquisition of development rights or scenic easements	2.88
21. Capital improvement program	2.53

Source: Godschalk et al. (1989).

[a]$N = 403$.

[b]Based on a five-point scale.

Development Management Tools and Techniques

Conventional Zoning

Conventional zoning ordinances control the type of land uses allowed in particular parts of a community (e.g., residential, commercial, industrial) as well as their intensity (e.g., bulk, height, floor-area ratio, setback provisions). Zoning ordinances can be very useful, then, in accomplishing a variety of local goals, for instance, to prohibit or reduce development in environmentally sensitive coastal lands (e.g., coastal wetlands, aquifer recharge zones, wellhead protection zones, maritime forests). These ordinances can be used to prohibit or restrict development in high-risk hazard zones, thus reducing exposure of people and property to hurricanes, riverine flooding, and other coastal hazards.

In addition to identifying permissible land uses, zoning ordinances also frequently stipulate a variety of performance controls or standards. These include, among others, setback standards (e.g., side yard and front yard setbacks), height restrictions, restrictions on the extent of impervious surfaces, and stormwater management requirements. In many ways, there has been a substantial "greening" of traditional zoning ordinances in recent years with greater attention paid to managing development in ways which minimize environmental degradation. For instance, open space and recreational uses may be the most appropriate activities to be permitted in high-risk areas, such as ocean erodible zones and NFIP V zones. Restricting such areas to commercial or public recreational activities would substantially reduce the amount of property at risk and in turn the property losses to accrue from future hurricanes and storms.

Zoning, with its emphasis on separation of uses, predictability of land development, and regulation of building height, bulk, and land area is the most common regulatory device for guiding coastal development. Zoning has been upheld as constitutional and a legitimate exercise of the police power since the U.S. Supreme Court decision in *City of Euclid v. Ambler Realty Co.*, 272 U.S. 365 (1926), but the application of specific provisions is still subject to challenge. In North Carolina, for instance, the Supreme Court has held that a zoning ordinance is valid unless "it has no foundation in reason and is a merely arbitrary or irrational exercise of power having no substantial relation to the public health, the public morals, the public safety, or the public welfare in its proper sense."

Zoning can and has been very useful to many oceanfront communities in reducing or keeping density down in high-risk shorefront locations. The town of Nags Head, North Carolina has changed beachfront zoning to reduce the extent of high-density development, hence reducing the risk to lives and the tax base.

Setback Requirements

The concept of a development setback has long been a part of zoning and is an especially important regulatory element in many coastal communities. Setbacks are used in urban settings to ensure that sufficient land is available for future roads and other public improvements and to ensure adequate light, access, and separation of structures. Setbacks in coastal hazard areas are an extension of this zoning technique and have become relatively common as a means of minimizing the impact of development on beach and dune systems and reducing exposure to storm hazards (e.g., Kusler et al., 1982; University of North Carolina, 1984). Such setbacks may be state-mandated or local option. As we have seen, North Carolina's CAMA requires small coastal developments to be located landward of the first line of vegetation, a distance of 30 times the annual rate of erosion for that segment of coast. In the case of multi-family structures and structures of more than 5,000 square feet in size, the setback is 60 times the annual rate of erosion.

The city of Myrtle Beach, South Carolina, is a good example of such an oceanfront setback. It has adopted a retreat policy and has delineated a 50-year erosion line to implement the policy. Only certain limited uses are allowed seaward of the line (e.g., sundecks, patios, gazebos, walkways).

Community Character

Zoning ordinances are also used by many coastal localities to protect community character. The town of Canon Beach, Oregon, for example, has included in its zoning ordinance several provisions intended to preserve the community's image as an artist colony and to protect the small-town coastal feeling that attracts tourists each year. Among other things, the town's zoning code specifically prohibits drive-in and "formula food" restaurants. The latter are defined in the code as any restaurant "required by contractual or other arrangements to offer standardized menus, ingredients, food preparation, interior or exterior design or uniforms" (Beatley et al., 1988). Excluded, then, are the likes of McDonalds and Pizza Huts. The town has also created a special design review board which imposes certain design standards on new development. (Hilton Head, S.C., imposes similar design standards.) The town of Nantucket, Massachusetts, is another example of a coastal community imposing architectural design standards in an effort to protect the integrity of the town's historic architecture.

Subdivision Ordinances

Subdivision regulations govern the conversion of raw land into building sites and the type and extent of improvement made in this conversion. Subdivision regulations can control the configuration and layout of development. They can also establish effective requirements and standards for public improvements, including streets, drainage pipes, sewer outlets, and so forth. The requirement of minimum lot size, although usually done in the zoning ordinance, can reduce the amount of new development exposed to storm hazards. Site plan review and other requirements of subdivision approval can provide the opportunity to encourage the location of development sites in ways which minimize storm risks. For instance, subdivision regulations may require that new single-family dwellings on lots in hazard areas be sited so as to maximize the distance from high-hazard oceanfront areas.

Dedication or reservation of recreation areas adequate to serve the residents of the immediate neighborhood within the subdivision is often required. Dedications of a specified amount of land (usually for parks or schools) or money in lieu of land force the developer of the subdivision to provide for needs generated by the subdivision. When the developer is allowed to pay in cash instead of in land, the community is given additional flexibility in meeting the needs of the subdivision. If, for example, a good park site is not available on the land owned by a developer, the cash contribution can allow the local government to purchase a nearby park site for the neighborhood.

Subdivision approval might also be made contingent on mitigation actions such as the protection of dunes, wetlands, or natural vegetation. For instance, subdivision provisions may require that structures be located a sufficient distance from protective dunes. Subdivision approvals may also be made contingent upon the planting of certain vegetation and the restoration and repair of existing dunes. Another promising alternative is to preserve the option of moving a structure back from the ocean by requiring lots which are sufficiently deep for this purpose. The additional depth could be considered analogous to the "repair" areas often required for septic tank use. If necessary, a structure could then be moved to the landward portion of the lot, in a safer location.

While traditional zoning and subdivision controls are in relatively common usage in coastal areas, as Table 8.1 indicates, there are major concerns about their ability to effectively promote local sustainability. In the following sections we describe some of the limitations of traditional land use controls and more recent trends and innovations which respond to these concerns.

Critique of Conventional Zoning and Subdivision Control   Traditional zoning and subdivision controls have come under increasing criticism in recent years. "Euclidean zoning," in its traditional effort at classifying and sharply separating different uses, is increasingly seen as inflexible, rigid, and promoting inefficient and undesirable land use patterns. Fixed in early thinking that certain noxious commercial and industrial uses (e.g., the tannery or noisy factory) must be kept separate and isolated from residential uses, conventional zoning has created land use patterns which virtually require automobile use, work against pedestrian orientation, and reduce social interaction and the integration of uses and activities viewed today as important ingredients in the livability of cities and towns. Such rigid land use controls, moreover, discourage creative land development and design.

Conventional zoning and subdivision controls are also criticized for how they function in newly urbanized and suburbanizing locations. In many coastal localities it is common to require 5- or 10-acre-minimum lot sizes. The objective is to protect the coastal character and to minimize the need for public facilities and other public investments. What often results, however, is a wasteful consumption of coastal land, allowing or requiring that such areas be carved up that much faster because of the minimum lot size.

In many coastal areas, however, larger lots may be legitimately mandated for environmental protection reasons—for instance, to reduce the amount of nonpoint source runoff and the number of on-site septic tanks, etc.

It is perhaps paradoxical that in such sensitive environmental locations keeping density down through such large-lot requirements may lead to a pattern of unsightly development, wasteful land consumption, and loss of coastal open space. This is a trade-off that local coastal officials must grapple with. It is important to recognize, however, that even where density must, for environmental or ecological reasons, be kept to a minimum there may well be other land use control techniques available that do not create such development patterns—for instance, development clustering, acquisition of sensitive lands, and transfer of development rights (all discussed below). It is also important to understand that it is not the tool *per se* that produces desired or undesired results, it is how that tool is used.

Urban Growth Boundaries A common criticism of American urban growth patterns is that there is usually no sharp or clear separation between urban and rural areas. Urban development sprawls into the countryside and important agricultural and natural resource areas. Commercial development tends to follow highways and major roads, leading to the pejorative description "strip commercial." As we have seen, traditional land use controls may not prevent coastal sprawl, and indeed may facilitate it.

A few cities and towns around the country are experimenting with the use of urban growth boundaries (UGBs), which limit the spatial extent of urban development and growth and seek to promote a more compact and contiguous urban growth pattern. As yet there are few notable examples of coastal communities that have employed the UGB concept, but the state of Oregon mandates the adoption of UGBs by all incorporated communities. Under Oregon's statewide growth management system (Senate Bill 100), cities must delineate an UGB (through negotiation with counties) that includes a sufficient supply of land to accommodate approximately 20 years of growth. Major public facility expenditures (e.g., for sewers and water) can only occur within the UGB, and major residential development projects are not permitted outside UGBs. One example of a coastal community employing the UGB, in combination with other management tools, is Canon Beach, Oregon.

The UGB concept can be an important tool, then, for coastal localities seeking to promote more efficient, less land-consumptive development patterns. In redirecting growth and activity inward, such a technique may also have the advantage of helping to reinvigorate existing towns and communities and provide a critical cross of people and development to support a variety of cultural amenities, businesses, vibrant and active public spaces, etc.

Some coastal communities have sought to use these and other techniques to support and sustain traditional village growth patterns. The island of Nantucket is an example of such an effort, only somewhat successful, however. The island town experienced a major real estate boom in the mid- to late-1980s. Much of this growth occurred in a large-lot, sprawl fashion. The town's *Goals and Objectives for Balanced Growth* (1990) states its desire to control this pattern and the resulting destruction of open space. It is the objective of the town

> To create a land use management system designed to guide future development into or near designated "growth areas" consistent with the Island's historical settlement pattern and within reach of infrastructure, while discouraging development in designated "low-growth areas." (p. 16)

Coastal localities may need to consider a host of other related changes in policy to help bring about growth containment, if this is a desired goal. Sufficient and necessary public services, facilities, and other public investments must occur in designated growth areas, and restrictions on any substantial building outside of these areas must also be enacted. Other policies might include eliminating the prohibition (quite common) on accessory units (or "granny flats") in residential areas, identifying existing vacant infill development sites and promoting new development in these areas, permitting and encouraging adaptive reuse of sites and buildings in already existing towns and communities, and allowing for and promoting the mixing and integration of different land uses (e.g., commercial, residential, etc.).

Redirecting growth back toward existing city and town centers has many potential payoffs, including increased economic vitality, a greater supply of affordable housing, more efficient provision of services and facilities, creation of more vital and livable urban spaces, and protection of coastal open space and sensitive lands. Efforts of older port communities to revitalize their waterfronts and rejuvenate their downtowns represent positive moves toward coastal sustainability. Baltimore's Harborplace is one of the most successful examples of such an effort.

Clustering or "Creative" Development Another increasingly mandated requirement is the *clustering* of development. Clustering may either be required generally or be presented to developers as an option. Applied either way, these provisions do not affect the overall density permitted on a particular site but instead seek to concentrate or cluster a higher density of structures on portions of the site. By directing density to a particular portion of a site, clustering can both permit and encourage development to locate on the less-hazardous portions of a site, while preserving hazard-prone or more sensitive areas in an undeveloped state.

A prime opportunity for accomplishing such a reorientation of development could occur during reconstruction following a damaging storm. For instance, post-storm development regulations could encourage clustering new development on the landward side of the ocean highway, with parking and recreational open space areas on the seaward side. Undeveloped beachfront areas may typically include features such as wetlands or vegetation, which in themselves serve to protect against storm forces. Clustering may also encourage the construction of buildings that are more structurally resistant to storm forces. Clustering can also economize on the public facilities, such as sewer, water, and roads, which must accompany development, in turn reducing the amount of property at risk.

Traditional Neighborhood Development Considerable attention has been paid in recent years to revisiting the qualities and characteristics of the traditional American town, and attempting to encourage new development which embodies and reflects these characteristics. Among these qualities are an orientation toward walking (and less emphasis on the automobile), a mixing of different uses (i.e., residential, commercial), incorporation of a public or civic realm (e.g., public squares and open space, civic buildings), and clustering of development around town centers. Architects Andres Duany and Elizabeth Plater-Zyberk are often credited with popularizing the notion of "neotraditional" planning, and have been instrumental in designing a number of neo-traditional communities, the best known among these is Seaside, Florida.

Proponents of neotraditionalism (recently relabeled by some as "new urbanism") are critical of traditional American zoning and development codes, which often impose rigid and inflexible development standards. Such codes typically require the sharp separation of uses (so-called Euclidean zoning), mandate minimum street and parking requirements favoring auto use, and encourage large-lot conventional (cul-de-sac) style development patterns. Increasingly, to overcome such rigidity, localities are adopting traditional neighborhood development (TND) ordinances, which allow greater flexibility in the layout and design of projects.

Neotraditional towns also have substantial potential to protect the natural environment and minimize the consumption of land in the development process. In the design of Seaside, for instance, most of the town is set well back from the Gulf of Mexico, with a wide strip along the beach preserved in an undeveloped state as open space. The pedestrian orientation and mixing of uses have the potential to substantially reduce auto usage, with accompanying reductions in air pollution, energy consumption, etc. In scaling back on the width and extent of roads and parking lots, such development patterns have the potential to be much less costly.

Bonus or Incentive Zoning   Bonus or incentive zoning allows developers to exceed limitations, usually height or density limitations, imposed by the zoning ordinance in exchange for developer-supplied amenities or concessions. For example, a builder may be permitted to exceed a height restriction if he or she provides open space adjacent to the proposed building. Incentive zoning has been used for some time in large urban developments. In New York, for example, a developer may obtain a 20% increase in permissible floor area for projects which incorporate a legitimate theater. Density bonuses have been given to encourage the incorporation of low- and moderate-income housing into development projects (Fox and Davis, 1978). In the case of coastal hazard areas, developers may be granted additional development units if projects incorporate hazard-reduction features. These features may include the dedication of sensitive coastal lands, for example, or the provision of design features that increase the ability of structures to withstand storm forces.

Hilton Head, South Carolina, has employed density bonuses for several years in exchange for dune restoration, beach access, and improvements in neighborhood drainage (Beatley et al., 1988).

Critics of density bonuses sometimes express concern that the traded mitigation and design amenities do not make up for the negatives of increased density. While an oceanfront development project may provide, for instance, additional drainage improvements, it can be argued that the increased number of people and property now at risk to a coastal storm make the outcome a questionable one. Density bonuses will tend to be the most successful where the added density occurs in especially desirable locations (e.g., an existing town center where additional density may even be seen as a positive contribution).

Performance Zoning Performance zoning sets standards for each zone based on permissible effects of a development rather than specifically enumerating the types of uses, dimensions, or densities permitted. If the prescribed standards are met, any development is allowed in the zone. This technique has been extensively used in industrial zoning to set limits on noise, dust, noxious emissions, and glare. More recently, the technique has been used in broader applications, with standards keyed to demands on public services such as water supply, wastewater treatment, and roads. Application may involve protection of the environment by specifying maximum levels of permissible stress on natural systems. For example, a community may specify the amount of permissible disturbance of vegetation in a given zone, and any use would have to meet that standard before development could take place. Performance controls for sensitive lands may work as a system to protect natural processes in environmentally sensitive areas, such as wetlands, floodplains, and dune systems.

Planned Unit Developments A number of coastal jurisdictions have adopted special provisions to allow planned unit developments (PUDs). PUDs combine elements of zoning and subdivision regulation in permitting flexible design of large- and small-scale developments which are planned and built as a unit. Specific plans for the development are required in advance and must be approved by the administrative body. This concept eliminates the lot-by-lot approach common to zoning and subdivision regulation and can be used as an incentive for better development by enabling complete development proposals to be planned and approved.

In its simplest form, planned unit development takes the shape of cluster development. An example might involve a developer with 100 acres of land, which he could divide into 400 quarter-acre lots as a matter of right according to existing local ordinances. Cluster zoning would give the developer the alternative of clustering units closer together in one part of the site, provided that the overall number of units does not exceed 400. The open space saved by clustering is left for the common use of the residents. From this simple "density transfer," planned unit development builds into complex forms. In its most advanced stage, PUD allows a variety of housing types as well as commercial, agricultural, and industrial uses. Typically, developers are permitted to develop under PUD provisions when the proposed development exceeds a minimum specified number of acres or housing units. Planned unit developments are usually subject to zoning ordinances, although they are not actually mapped, and must therefore comply with the use restrictions within the zones where they occur. Increasingly, however, some mixing of uses and expansion of density are permitted.

The PUD technique provides flexibility because the final design is a matter of negotiation between the developers and the planning authorities. PUDs are generally attractive to developers of large tracts of land. These projects can often be provided with urban services and facilities more economically than conventional development. They also allow environmental protection of sensitive areas while providing for residential and commercial development. PUD project design can enhance storm hazard reduction requirements when the developer's plans incorporate features such as protective land and vegetation buffers and the provision of on-site storm shelters.

Carrying Capacity

The possibility of tying permitted new growth to the capacity of a coastal locality and its residents to respond to a storm hazard is a well-known use of carrying capacity. Such an approach has been employed in the growth management system adopted by Sanibel Island, Florida.

Shortly after the island was incorporated, a comprehensive plan based explicitly on the capacity of the island's natural and built environments to sustain new growth was developed. Evacuation of the island was calculated to take five hours, assuming 12 hours of warning and subtracting from that a four-hour hazard cutoff time (beyond which evacuation is not possible) and a three-hour mobilization time (i.e., time required for warning, preparation of residents, and for establishing an evacuation system). The capacity of the island was thus the number of people who could evacuate in that time.

Carrying capacity means the natural and manmade limits to development beyond which significant harm will occur. Carrying capacity can be used to assess the effects of development on such natural factors as groundwater supply and wetlands productivity and manmade factors such as sewage treatment and roadway capacity. This concept has been applied in practice to a number of coastal localities. Several implications for storm hazard reduction arise from the application of carrying capacity analysis. The first is that, as in Sanibel, carrying capacity is particularly relevant to assessing evacuation capacity. Second, natural and manmade limitations on coastal development may provide a rational means to regulate the location and quantity of new growth, which in turn may serve to reduce storm hazards. Carrying capacity objectives, in other words, may be used to reinforce and compliment efforts to reduce storm hazards generally.

Land and Property Acquisition

The acquisition of land and property, or interests therein, may in many cases be a very effective approach to achieving a variety of coastal objectives, from hazard reduction to reduction of nonpoint sources to conservation of coastal open space. Several acquisition approaches are discussed here: (1) fee-simple acquisition of undeveloped land, (2) acquisition of less-than-fee-simple interests in undeveloped land, and (3) fee-simple acquisition or relocation of existing development.

Fee-Simple Acquisition of Undeveloped Land   Fee-simple acquisition involves obtaining the full "bundle of rights" associated with a parcel of real property. With respect to local sustainability, land acquisition may have several functions. The first is to secure for the public certain lands, especially those that are sensitive, vulnerable, or hazardous and which should not be developed. A large-scale public acquisition of land can serve to influence the direction and timing of development in a locality. Urban land banking programs, particularly popular in Europe, have attempted to regulate growth by preventing development in some locations while strategically releasing other land more desirable for development. Land acquisition can also be used to secure, in advance and typically at lower prices, land that will be needed at some point in the future for public facilities and services.

The use of fee-simple acquisition as a coastal management tool poses a number of practical questions. Perhaps the most significant problem is the cost and means of financing acquisitions. Outright purchase of land in coastal areas experiencing moderate or high levels of market demand will tend to be very expensive—prohibitively so for many localities.

There are several examples of coastal communities that have successfully employed fee-simple acquisition. Nantucket's Land Bank is one of the best examples. Created in 1984 in response to a growth boom and the attendant loss of open space, the bank is funded through a 2% real estate transfer tax (paid at closing by the buyer). This funding source has proven to be an effective way of generating a sizable level of funding, and is probably much more politically feasible than many other possible sources (e.g., raising local property taxes).

The Nantucket Land Bank is independent of the town and is governed by a commission. In addition to its power to impose the land transfer tax, the bank also has the power to float bonds, which it has recently done, in order to acquire as much land as possible before it is lost to development. The acquisition program will do much to help the island preserve its natural environment (e.g., the moors and hearthlands) and may prove to be one of the most effective growth management tools for promoting more traditional village-oriented growth patterns.

The positive Nantucket experience has spawned land acquisition initiatives in other locations (e.g., Martha's Vineyard, Mass.; Little Compton, R.I.; and Hilton Head, S.C.).

Acquisition of Development Rights   Where the fee-simple purchase of hazardous lands is, for various reasons, not feasible, the purchase of less-than-fee-simple interests in land may work. One such approach is to acquire just certain rights to develop environmentally sensitive, high-hazard, or other lands that should not be developed. Under this arrangement, rather than fee-simple title, a local government would pay the landowner the fair market value of just those rights in exchange for agreeing to leave the land in an undeveloped state for a specified period of time (but often in perpetuity). The transaction is usually accomplished through a restrictive covenant attached to the property.

As with fee-simple acquisition, a number of practical questions arise. First, in what manner are development rights to be acquired? Does the jurisdiction use its powers of eminent domain or does it simply negotiate with willing sellers on the open market for the development rights? This question may have significant implications for the ability of the purchase of development rights (PDR) to protect large blocks of sensitive coastal land. For instance, relying on voluntary sales may permit, even encourage, substantial development in an adjacent undeveloped sensitive area, thus doing little more than shift new development from some parcels to other parcels within the area. Through the use of eminent domain over the entire area, this potential "checkerboard effect" can be prevented.

There is, as well, the question of exactly which development rights are being purchased by a locality. The greater the economic use that stays with the property owner, the greater will be the parcel's remaining fair market value and hence the less costly will be the development rights. Exactly which uses are permitted after development rights have been purchased may also influence overall property at risk in other areas. For instance, if private recreational activities are permitted, this may in turn induce further residential and other development in adjacent areas where development rights have not been purchased. These types of development influences and side effects should be considered when defining the rights to be purchased and the types of uses and activities that will be permitted.

PDR can be used effectively in collaboration with development regulation. On the one hand, restricting development in a particularly sensitive area of the jurisdiction may prevent the checkerboard effect that sometimes results from a voluntary PDR. In turn, PDR may serve to soften the economic effects of development regulations and reduce as well the political oppositions typically engendered by regulatory programs.

While not widely used, the prime example of PDR has been in protecting farmland. Suffolk County, New York, King County, Washington, and the state of Connecticut have used the PDR concept to protect farmland (Duncan, 1984).

As an alternative to the purchase of development rights, a coastal locality could encourage the donation of scenic or conservation easements. Landowners can be encouraged to make such donation in large part because of the income tax deductions permissible under the Internal Revenue Code.

Transfer of Development Rights   One potentially effective approach to managing coastal development patterns is the transfer of development rights (TDR). TDR is an innovative approach to development management which is being used in only a few places in the country (Carmichael, 1974; Costonis, 1973; Rose, 1975; Merriam, 1978). The basic concept underlying TDR is that ownership of land includes a right to develop the land, a right which may be separated from other ownership rights and transferred to someone else. For example, under a TDR system, an owner may sell this development right to another property owner, who under the TDR system must collect a specified number of development rights before developing his or her property at the desired density.

Commentators have theorized that the use of TDR can substantially eliminate the value shifts and inequities of zoning by allowing the market to compensate owners who under a normal zoning scheme would have the development potential of their land restricted with no compensation (Rose, 1975; Merriam, 1978). A TDR system can be either voluntary or mandatory. Under the latter, a locality would simply zone open space or sensitive coastal lands so that development would not be allowed, and the owner of land within this zone would then be permitted to transfer all or some of this unused development density to parcels in designated development areas or to sell the development rights on the open market to others who own land in areas designated for development. The locality would then permit increased levels of development in the receiving zone as a result of possessing extra development rights, thus creating a natural market for the transferable development rights. A voluntary approach would simply present the transfer as an additional option for the landowner—a way of maintaining the land in its undeveloped state if the landowner wishes. The landowner in this case would still have the option of developing his or her land or selling it for development purchases.

The TDR approach raises a number of sticky practical issues. First, there are several alternative institutional arrangements for operating a TDR program. On one hand, the transfer of development rights can be left entirely to market dynamics, with the locality only involved in designating sending and receiving zones and determining the number of rights to be transferred. Whether a selling landowner receives a fair price for his or her rights will depend simply on what the market will provide. While there are policy decisions which must be made in the initial allocation of rights, the local government adopts an essentially hands-off stance once the system is created. An alternative institutional structure would have the jurisdiction play a more direct and active role in the development rights transaction itself, perhaps serving as a broker—buying and selling rights as needed. This in turn helps to ensure that an adequate price is obtained, thereby overcoming short-term market fluctuations. While the latter approach would permit greater control over the price and quantity of rights sold, it would also require greater government expense and oversight. An intermediate position might permit the local government to enter the market at occasional critical points while leaving the bulk of development rights transfers to the dynamics of the local market.

Another difficulty is devising a methodology for assigning rights. They might be allocated strictly according to acreage (e.g., one right per acre) or to the market value of the property. Eventually the question will arise as to whether additional rights should be allocated. If new supplies of development rights are needed, a practical and fair procedure for allocating additional TDRs must be devised.

The locality must also decide how rights transferred from sending zones can be used. If a developer purchases 10 development rights from land in a sensitive area and seeks to apply them in a receiving zone, what rights is he or she entitled to? Each additional TDR, for example, might translate into a certain amount of additional floorspace or square footage allowed in the receiving zone. In the case of residential development, these additions may be measured in terms of additional dwelling units or bedrooms.

The use of TDRs can also be viewed as a form of compensation when restrictions are placed on development in storm hazard areas. For instance, although an oceanfront landowner may be prevented from developing his or her land (by an open-space or recreational-zoning classification), he or she may be able to realize a portion of its development potential by transferring allocated development rights to areas of the jurisdiction less environmentally sensitive or important. Viewing TDR as primarily a form of compensation raises several questions; chief among them is the extent of compensation deemed to be desirable or equitable. At what point will the market value of a development right be unacceptably low as a form of compensation? If full or substantial compensation is a goal, this may require a more active role for government in the development rights market, say, by entering the market to buy rights at times when demand is low.

A large-scale TDR program requires extensive information and knowledge about local market conditions and land development trends, and this can represent a major limitation. For example, how large should the receiving zone be, and by how much should the locality raise permissible densities to ensure an adequate demand for development rights? How readily will landowners in sending zones sell their development rights and under what conditions? One reasonable approach to these empirical limitations is to develop a modest TDR pilot program, with relatively small receiving and sending zones which can be monitored closely over time.

Taxation and Fiscal Incentives

The specific management provisions included in this broad category are designed primarily to affect indirectly the quantity and type of development to occur in sensitive coastal lands. In contrast to the public acquisition of land, a taxation policy might seek to reduce development in certain areas by decreasing the holding costs of open space and vacant land, in turn reducing the opportunity costs of not developing such lands for more intensive uses. While taxation and fiscal policy can encompass numerous specific tools and mechanisms, attention is primarily focused on differential property taxation and special assessments and impact fees.

Differential Taxation   The use of differential taxation is based on the theory that, by reducing the property tax burden on undeveloped parcels of land, pressures to convert the parcels to more intensive uses will be reduced by decreasing holding costs and increasing the profitability of current uses. Almost every state now has provisions for some form of preferential assessment (Coughlin and Keene, 1981; Keene et al., 1976). The uses which are typically eligible for property tax relief are farm and forestland, open space, and recreational uses.

Three basic variations of differential assessment are currently in use: pure preferential assessment, deferred taxation, and restrictive agreements (Keene et al., 1976). Under the first type of program, preferred land uses are assessed, for local property tax purposes, not at their fair market value (i.e., the potential development value) but rather at their value in their current uses. If the land is in farmland, for instance, it is assessed according to its agricultural use value, usually based on a state-determined capitalization formula. If after several years of receiving the lower assessment the benefited landowner decides to develop the land, he or she is still permitted to do so without having to repay the property taxes foregone as a result of the use-value assessment. In contrast to this pure approach is that of deferred taxation. The difference here is that the landowner changing the use of his or her land is required to repay a portion of the tax benefits received. However, the recapture period is typically not very long, with five years perhaps the average. In addition, most states using this approach require the landowner to pay interest on the recaptured fund, usually at a below-market rate. A third approach, the use of restrictive agreements, is best exemplified by California's Williamson Act (Gustafson and Wallace, 1975). Here, in order for qualifying landowners to obtain lower tax assessments, they must be willing to enter into written agreements to keep their land in its current use for a minimum period of 10 years. This contract is a "rolling-front" agreement which is self-renewing each year unless the landowner explicitly notifies the locality of an intention to change the use. There are also provisions which permit the landowner to break the contract subject to certain penalties.

While differential taxation has been used in most states as a technique to preserve farmland, its effectiveness at retaining land in undeveloped uses is generally found to be low. Preferential assessment may indeed reduce holding costs somewhat or even substantially, but in the face of high market prices, and thus high opportunity costs of maintaining land in open space, the pressures to develop will generally far outweigh the tax incentives (Dressler, 1979; Duncan, 1984). Consequently, differential assessment is likely to be most successful in situations where development pressures are slight to moderate and where landowners are actively interested in maintaining the present undeveloped use of the land.

Differential assessment will also be a more effective tool when used in collaboration with other approaches, such as the regulation of new development, the fee-simple purchase of land, and the transfer of development rights. For instance, reducing the permissible development density in a hazardous location, together with preferential assessment, may reduce opportunity costs to the landowner enough to reduce actual conversion of hazard lands to developed uses.

To maximize the effects of these tax benefits, a locality could consider establishing mechanisms for funneling tax benefits to those lands with the greatest protection or conservation value. This might entail, for example, the reduction of local assessments/rates of taxation in excess of what is provided under uniform state differential assessment provisions, thus providing greater tax benefits for parcels of open space, forest, and farmland of special value.

Special Assessments and Impact Fees   People who build in and inhabit sensitive coastal areas (e.g., high-risk hazard zones) often impose substantially greater costs on the public than those who dwell elsewhere. These costs are realized when a hurricane or coastal storm strikes or threatens to strike a locality. Here there are public costs of evacuation, search and rescue, temporary housing, debris clearance, and the reconstruction of public facilities such as roads, utilities, water and sewer lines, and so on. One public policy approach is to acknowledge that additional public expenses will be entailed by permitting development in certain hazardous areas and to assess those who will ultimately benefit from the expenditures. This approach can be accomplished through several means.

One technique is to attempt to tie more closely benefits received and costs incurred through the use of special benefit assessments. A special assessment, while not technically a tax, is a method of raising revenue in which all or part of the cost of a facility (such as a road improvement, sewer, or water system) is charged to a property owner who is so situated in relation to the facility as to derive a special benefit from the improvement. The tax charged each property owner is usually proportionate to the frontage along which the facility abuts his or her property, the area of the land served by the improvement, or the value added to the land served by the project. Special assessments are typically confined to a geographical district in which property owners are determined to receive a direct and substantial benefit in excess of the general benefits received by the public at large (Hagman and Misczynski, 1979).

To apply the special assessment concept to storm hazard management, a locality would designate an area in which "special storm services" are provided and in which residents would be subject to the special assessment. This approach raises a number of issues. The first is how the extent of the special assessment is determined and justified. Imposing a special assessment may require a number of assumptions, and rather rough estimates, about exactly what public costs are associated with an actual or potential hurricane. The magnitude of these costs will, of course, depend on the assumed size and severity of the storm event, among other things. It would also be difficult to determine what special storm services would be needed, on whom the special assessment should be levied, and on what basis the assessment is calculated—an *ad valorem* property tax or a levy on the number of dwelling units.

A variation on the theme of requiring private parties who impose public costs to pay for them is the *impact fee*, which are increasingly popular with local governments around the country. In theory, the impact fee levy is designed to recoup and mitigate the overall "impacts" of a project or development on the community at large—impacts that may extend beyond the immediate environs and requirements of a discrete project or development. For instance, while a special assessment may be levied to cover the immediate costs associated with the floodproofing of sewer and water service, an impact fee would cover broader and more diffuse consequences of development in a hazardous area that are less clearly related to services or benefits received directly by a specific site or development. An impact fee is not designed to cover the costs of a specific improvement by which a particular development will reap a special benefit, but it is designed to require the developer (and future residents who purchase these properties) to compensate the public for the additional costs of these consequences.

The impact fee may be instituted as a separate instrument or, more typically, attached to the exactions process during development review and approval (Hagman and Misczynski, 1979). In some states, the impact fee may also represent a way of getting around legislative and court-imposed limitations on the extent of exactions permissible (e.g., restricted to the installation of roads, sewers, and other facilities, or the donation of open space, school sites, and other land) (Stroud, 1978). The impact fee holds promise as a formal procedure for calculating and assessing impacts which may present a greater level of certainty for developers than currently exists under the highly negotiated exaction process. Adjusting the expectations of the development community and creating a relatively clear and consistent set of public safety and environmental management obligations may well be an important local objective.

Capital Facilities and Public Infrastructure Policy

Coastal development—its type, location, density, and timing—is highly influenced by capital facilities such as roads, sewers, and water services. Such public investments have been aptly termed "growth shapers." In this section we will briefly review the potential role to be played by the location, type, and timing of capital facilities in managing coastal development. Issues relating to the financing of these facilities have been discussed in a general way in the earlier section on taxation and financial incentives. The use of particular pricing policies may also significantly affect patterns of development, but this strategy is not discussed here.

Policies to Prevent Location of Public Facilities in Sensitive or High-Risk Areas   There are two primary dimensions of public investment in capital facilities which have implications for local management; one is geographical, where capital facilities are placed, and the other is temporal, when they are put in place. With respect to the first dimension, a locality can develop an explicit set of capital facilities extension policies designed, for instance, to avoid high-hazard areas, thus reducing the amount of development and property attracted to the area and the potential threats to lives and property. This approach can only become an effective deterrent, however, if development in such areas is dependent upon (or deems highly attractive) the existence of public facilities. If, as is often the case in resort areas, coastal development is able to obtain water through individual site wells and dispose of wastewater through septic tanks, a reorienting of sewer and water facilities by the locality will do little to impede growth in undesirable locations. It may then be necessary for the locality to foreclose other service/facility options available to developers by, for example, restricting the issuance of septic tank permits. But without valid health reasons, foreclosing such alternative options for development may be legally problematic.

The use of public infrastructure policy in order to restrict or direct the growth of a city, however, may be subject to a variety of legal challenges. Within the city limits, a city may be required to provide equal service to all its residents once it provides a service to any of them. The city may extend utility services beyond the city limits, but only within reasonable limits and for the public benefit. The city, when considering the extension of services beyond its limits, must consider the amount of territory to be serviced, its distance from the city, and the effect that the extension will have on customers' rates and the city's capital debt structure. If the city extends services beyond the city limits, it has some discretionary power to condition the provision of the services. The agreement to provide extraterritorial services is contractual in nature, subject to the usual rules of bargain and contract. Rates may be higher for extraterritorial customers.

Redirecting capital facilities, and the development which accompanies them, into safer or more desirable areas of the locality can be facilitated through several means. One is the clear delineation of an urban services area in which the jurisdiction agrees to provide certain facilities or services. The service district might also entail a temporal dimension, including sufficient land to accommodate 10 or 20 years of future growth under various assumptions (as discussed in the earlier section entitled Urban Growth Boundaries).

The urban services area technique has several advantages. It provides a long-term perspective on growth and development and permits developers, residents, and the local government to visualize where and when public facilities will become available in the future, and where they cannot be expected. This, in effect, modifies long-term expectations about where future development will and will not be acceptable to the community. Development pressures may tend to shift naturally as a result of this public designation, as developers, landowners, and others realize that certain facilities will be made available outside the designated areas. However, restriction of public facilities, which curtails the overall amount of development that take place in a community, may raise suspicions of "no-growth" objectives. Consequently, the local government should make a good faith effort to designate a service area in safer, less sensitive, and more desirable areas within the locality sufficient to satisfy growth demands, so as to enhance the political and legal acceptability of the urban service area approach.

In more intermediate terms, the locality needs a policy instrument by which to systematically identify, finance, and sequence specific capital improvements. This is generally the function of a capital improvement program (CIP). Ideally, the CIP follows closely designated service boundaries, as well as the comprehensive plan, zoning, and other regulatory and planning provisions. The CIP provides a specific framework for making short-term (annual) decisions about which improvements to make and where. Avoidance storm hazard areas can easily be incorporated into this instrument and decision framework as a specific CIP policy.

A close connection between the designation of service areas, the capital improvement program, and the overall planning process (including the local comprehensive plan) in a jurisdiction is essential. Such a close function linkage will tend to enhance the combined effectiveness of each policy or technique in advancing overall local objectives and will emphasize their authority. From a practical standpoint, the concept of guiding growth through capital facilities should be closely linked to the objective of reducing the public costs of such facilities and the extent of public investment at risk to coastal hazards. The latter consideration is, by itself, a legitimate argument for denying facility extension into hazard areas and provides a sound legal rationale for a hazard-sensitive capital facilities extension policy.

Several recent hurricane hazard mitigation planning efforts illustrate the potential role of capital facilities in guiding growth into less hazardous coastal areas. The Surf City, North Carolina, hurricane hazard mitigation plan suggests the use of sewer service extensions as a means to divert growth to less hazardous areas of the locality:

> The Town should actively encourage development in the southern section of the town. Specifically, it is the area where

future high density development should be concentrated. Additionally, if an actual sewer system is developed in the near future, it should be designed to serve these areas rather than another section of the community where development in hazard areas would be encouraged by such a system. (Town of Surf City, N.C., 1984)

The hurricane hazard mitigation and reconstruction plan for the town of Nags Head contains similar recommendations, particularly in an attempt to discourage further growth in an incipient inlet area:

In the short term, the Town will explore the possibility of limiting future water service extension in the largely undeveloped area in the Whalebone incipient inlet area. While this does not preclude future growth, it ensures that the town will not be a willing participant in placing property at risk. (Town of Nags Head, N.C., 1984)

It should be remembered that public investments encompass more than sewers and roads, and include numerous structures and buildings from town halls to schools to police and fire stations. Again, it may be possible to locate these investments in areas less susceptible to storm forces, in turn serving to reduce the quantity of actual public property at risk and discouraging the location of other private development, and in ways which achieve other local objectives. By locating public structures in specific strategic location, and by constructing them to certain specifications, it may be possible to use them as storm shelters.

Relocation or Strengthening Capital Investments after Disaster Events Opportunities may exist after a hurricane or coastal storm has occurred to implement a community's capital facilities objectives. It may be possible, if the facilities are sufficiently damaged, that roads and sewers can be rebuilt in areas less susceptible to damage from the next storm. Even if the facilities are not relocated, they may be repaired and reconstructed in ways which make them stronger or less susceptible to storm forces. Roads and sewers can be elevated, for instance, and sewer and water lines can be floodproofed. Also, placing power and telephone lines underground after the storm will help ensure safer evacuation when the next storm threatens.

It may be possible as well that public facilities can be reconstructed in ways that not only reduce the possibility of their own damage but which reduce other storm-related hazards. As before, the presence of certain public facilities will influence development patterns. If certain facility repairs are not permitted to occur after a storm has hit, this may preclude or discourage the private redevelopment of the area. This technique was used subtly in the Baytown, Texas, case. The option of selling out and leaving the Brownwood Subdivision was made much more attractive to homeowners because they were uncertain that sewers and roads would be restored or maintained.

A similar approach might be taken with the rebuilding or reconstruction of damaged public buildings such as town halls and fire stations. If sufficiently damaged, it may be logical to move these structures to safer sites in the community. After Hurricane Camille, for instance, the Pass Christian Town Hall was rebuilt on higher ground and consequently was much more protected from future storm damage than if it would have been rebuilt in the same location. When structures are not relocated, it may be possible to repair or rebuild them in ways that reduce their susceptibility to future storm damage, such as through elevation. It may be desirable as well to rebuild public structures in ways which permit their usage as storm shelters.

Information Dissemination

Classical economic theory supposes that the more informed consumers are, the more rational and allocatively efficient their market decisions will be. This implies an additional set of local management strategies which aim primarily at supplementing and enlightening individual market decisions regarding the hurricane and storm threat. Several approaches can be taken in this vein.

The first approach is to seek mechanisms and processes which effectively inform potential buyers of the risks and physical characteristics associated with a particular area. Hazard information could be provided in several ways. Legislation might require that real estate agents inform prospective buyers about the potential dangers or risks. Prospective owners might be required to sign disclosure forms as a condition of receiving a development permit.

Whether such real estate disclosure provisions truly have any influence on the decisions of coastal developers or homeowners is questionable, however. This disclosure technique has been used in California in an attempt to inform prospective homebuyers of the risks of living near earthquake fault lines, and some evidence about effectiveness is available here. Under the Alquist-Priolo Special Studies Zones Act, a real estate agent or individual selling property must disclose to the prospective buyer the fact that the property lies in a "special studies zone" (earthquake fault zone). A study by Palm (1981) indicates, however, that this requirement has had little measurable effect on the market behavior of housing consumers. Among the problems identified are a tendency for homeowners to place a low priority in the earthquake threat, the issuance of the disclosure in the latter stages of a home purchase, a downplaying of the importance of the earthquake hazard zones, and a disclosure technique (a single line that says simply "in Alquist-Priolo zone") that conveys little or no real information about the earthquake risk. As Palm (1981, p. 102) observes, "At present, real estate agents are disclosing at the least sensitive time in the sales transaction, and are using methods which convey the least amount of information about special studies zones."

Consequently, if similar disclosure requirements are to be applied in coastal areas, the disclosure must be provided early in the sales transaction, preferably during the initial agent–purchaser meeting, and the disclosure must convey real and accurate information about the location and nature of coastal hazards. Not only should the disclosure form or process be labeled in a meaningful way (i.e., the home is in a "storm hazard zone" or "high-risk erosion zone," as opposed to an ambiguous "special studies zone"), it must provide a full description of the nature of the coastal risks. More passive types of hazard disclosure might also be useful. Included in this category are requirements that coastal hazard zone designations be recorded on deeds and subdivision plats and that public signs be erected indicating the boundaries of erosion or flood hazard areas (and perhaps the location of past storm damage). A number of coastal states and localities have used such passive approaches (and indeed is required under the NFIP).

Community Awareness Programs

A different approach is to institute programs which attempt to directly educate the housing consumer about coastal hazards. These programs might take the form of brochures and other materials distributed to new and prospective residents of the community, informing them of the nature and location of hazard zones and information about what to look for in a new home or business structure (such as elevation and floodproofing). For existing residents, this approach may be one of educating them about actions they can take to enhance the integrity of their existing structures (such as installing "hurricane clips") and reducing future property damages.

A locality might also attempt to disseminate hazard information on the "supply side." This technique might take the form of construction practice seminars for coastal builders and developers, introducing both conventional and innovative approaches to building and designing structures and to siting and planning the orientation of buildings in vulnerable locations. The success of such a strategy, however, depends essentially on the integrity of builders and developers, and those who are conscious and conscientious about storm threats are probably already planning their projects accordingly.

Impediments and Obstacles to Effective Local Management

While there is tremendous potential for effective coastal management at the local level, it is not always easy to develop, enact, and implement such programs. Table 8.3 presents further results from the 1984 study, specifically citing in rank order the perceived obstacles to the enactment of development management measures to address hurricane and coastal storm hazards in high-risk localities. As the table indicates, coastal localities will confront a host of impediments, including general conservative attitudes toward government control of private property rights, general feeling that the community can weather the storm, lack of financial resources, the existence of more pressing local problems and concerns, opposition of real estate and development interests, and lack of trained personnel. Similar problems of enforcement and implementation were highlighted in the survey results (Table 8.4).

Local officials will also likely confront several arguments against development management, including that such requirements will increase the costs of development, will dampen the local economy, and are illegal or unconstitutional (see Table 8.5). Local officials may also

TABLE 8.3

Obstacles to the Enactment of Development Management in Order of Frequency Cited

Obstacle	Frequency	Percentage	Importance index[a]
1. General conservative attitude toward government control of private property rights (*N*=359)	319	88.9	3.38
2. General feeling that community can weather the storm (*N*=357)	309	86.6	3.09
3. Lack of adequate financial resources to implement mitigation programs (*N*=347)	296	85.3	3.41
4. More pressing local problems and concerns (*N*=351)	291	82.9	3.28
5. Opposition of real estate and development interests (*N*=355)	286	80.6	3.06
6. Lack of trained personnel to develop mitigation programs (*N*=345)	278	80.6	2.91
7. Lack of incentives or requirements from higher levels of government (*N*=345)	278	80.6	3.02
8. Opposition of homeowners (*N*=338)	252	74.6	2.64
9. Opposition of business interests (*N*=337)	241	71.5	2.60
10. Absence of politically active individuals and groups advocating hurricane/storm mitigation (*N*=339)	242	71.4	2.85
11. Inadequate or inaccurate federal flood insurance maps (*N*=342)	215	62.9	2.49

Source: Godschalk et al. (1989).
[a]Based on a five-point scale.

TABLE 8.4

Problems in Enforcement and Implementation of Development Management Measures

Problem	Frequency	Percentage
1. Insufficient funds (N=195)	116	59.5
2. Public opposition (N=194)	89	45.9
3. Lack of support by public officials (N=192)	83	43.2
4. Lack of qualified personnel (N=195)	79	40.5
5. Insufficient database (N=195)	63	32.3

Source: Godschalk et al. (1989).

TABLE 8.5

Arguments against Enactment of Development in Order of Frequency

Arguments	Frequency	Percentage	Importance index[a]
1. Development management measures lead to increased developmental costs (N=368)	315	85.6	3.18
2. Decisions about risks from coastal storms are best left to the individual (N=346)	246	71.1	2.66
3. Development management measures dampen local economy (N=355)	245	69.0	2.52
4. Particular development management measures are illegal or unconstitutional (N=338)	225	66.6	2.42

Source: Godschalk et al. (1989).
[a] Based on a five-point scale

confront the argument that decisions about hurricane and coastal storm risks are best left to individuals. While such arguments against planning and management are generally unfounded, supporters and proponents of management must be prepared to address them.

The attitudes of residents and property owners in coastal areas and the general attraction of coastal living might also be thought of as obstacles to more sensible and sustainable development patterns. Recent

TABLE 8.6

Results of Questionnaire Administered to Owners of Beachfront Property Damaged by Hurricane Hugo [a]

Possible responses	Frequency	Percentage
1. Yes, would not buy beachfront property again	8	6.1
2. Yes, would like to sell my property and buy property in a safer location	9	6.8
3. No, hurricanes are just a normal risk in beach-front areas	52	39.3
4. No, the benefits and enjoyment of beachfront living outweigh the potential risks	55	41.7
5. Other	8	6.1

Source: Beatley (1992).

[a] The following question was asked of the property owners (N=132): "Now that you have experienced the effects of a hurricane, has this had any influence on your feelings about owning beachfront property?" (circle all that apply).

surveys of coastal property owners suggest that many of them do have a solid appreciation for the danger and riskiness of building and living in coastal areas but see hurricanes and coastal storms as simply a necessary part of the trade-off for the benefits of coastal living (Beatley, 1992). Table 8.6 represents the results of a mail questionnaire administered to owners of beachfront property in South Carolina heavily damaged by Hurricane Hugo. As the results indicate even those who have been devastated by such events do not generally have regrets or plan to move to safer locations. A related obstacle is the economic advantage of beachfront locations. A major reason why beachfront property owners are reluctant to relocate their structures (and are willing to wait until the structure has nearly collapsed in the surf) is that many rent their units, and rental incomes are substantially higher on the first-row beachfront than on more inland sites.

Conclusions

This chapter has examined coastal management at the local level—existing patterns and potential future directions. We have emphasized that coastal localities are often in the best position to formulate and implement coastal management programs and to move in the direction of sustainability. We offered some ideas about what constitutes, in our minds, a sustainable coastal community. We do not expect complete agreement on our proposed definition but see it as a starting point, from which local planners, elected officials, citizens, and others should begin to discuss and debate.

In reviewing the existing patterns of local management, it is clear that coastal localities are more likely to have adopted conventional planning measures, such as basic zoning and subdivision ordinances. While these measures can be useful in advancing a number of local objectives, there are many other tools, techniques, and strategies that are available and which coastal localities may wish to add to their arsenal in promoting sustainability.

A number of obstacles to effective local management were identified. While it will remain a real challenge for proponents of sustainable communities to seek to overcome these obstacles, we believe it is possible, and there are a sufficient number of impressive local efforts to illustrate the great potential of such local strategies.

9

Conclusions: Future Directions in U.S. Coastal Management

As data presented in Chapter 2 suggest, we are increasingly becoming a coastal nation, with coastal areas around the country continuing to grow in absolute and relative terms. We are drawn, it seems, to live and recreate in close proximity to sea and shore, despite the hazards and costs of doing so.

While coastal growth and development pressures in the United States are probably inevitable, the destructive and hazardous nature of these land use and development patterns need not be. This book has attempted to highlight some of the current and potential strategies and policies that can be utilized to minimize and reduce the impacts of such pressures. We have reviewed promising programs and strategies at each governmental level and can conclude that there already is in place a useful policy and management framework. We believe, however, that major improvements in this framework can and must occur in the years ahead if our fragile and irreplaceable coastal environments are to be protected.

Sustainable Coastal Development as the Primary Goal

We believe that in the future all coastal management decisions must assume sustainability as their primary and essential goals. Sustainability must be the centerpiece of coastal management efforts at federal, state, regional, and local levels. As we discussed previously, there are many meanings of sustainability and sustainable development, and contemporary definitions are fraught with subjectivity and ambiguity. We do believe that as much as anything, coastal management programs must imbue a *philosophy* or *perspective* of sustainability, even though its precise meaning may be open to debate. This would represent a major positive step in the future.

As the Brundtland report says, sustainable development is development which "meets the needs of the present without compromising the ability of future generations to meet their own needs" (1987, p. 2). In a more recent report the National Commission on the Environment defined sustainable development as

> a strategy for improving the quality of life while preserving the environmental potential for the future, of living off interest rather than consuming natural capital. Sustainable development mandates that the present generation must not narrow the choices of future generations but must strive to expand them by passing on an environment and an accumulation of resources that will allow its children to live at least as well as, and preferably better than, people today. Sustainable development is premised on living within the earth's means. (p. 2)

Sustainable coastal development, then, implies new respect for environmental and ecological limits, a goal of living off the ecological interest while protecting the principal, a new orientation toward the future and toward adopting a long-term planning and management timeframe. Sustainable development, though, implies concerns not simply about environmental and ecological systems, but about social sustainability as well. Sustainable coastal development implies an attempt to promote greater livability and an equitable and just distribution of resources and opportunities in the coastal zone.

The feasibility or practicality of achieving coastal sustainability might be questioned by some. As population and growth pressures continue to rise in coastal America, isn't sustainability that much harder to achieve? Probably so, yet we believe sustainability remains an important and central goal. What may be practically aspired to in coastal areas is development and land use patterns which are *less unsustainable*.

How then do we move coastal areas in the direction of greater sustainability and who (which actors and jurisdictions) should have responsibility? The existing coastal management framework in the

United States has developed and evolved in certain understandable ways. Primary responsibility for regulating and controlling coastal activities and land uses lies with states and, through delegation of authority, local governments. Day-to-day land use management and control resides with the latter. Yet, the fundamental national interest in the coastal zone implies a legitimate federal role in encouraging and facilitating sensible state and local management. Coastal management, then, must and should involve each governmental level. Each has an important and productive role to play. What follows are some concluding thoughts about the future direction of management activities and strategies at each governmental level.

Federal Coastal Management

The federal government has a serious and important role to play in the U.S. coastal management framework. The federal Coastal Zone Management Act (CZMA) has, since the early 1970s, served as an important catalyst for the development of state coastal management programs as well as regional and local management efforts. The financial and technical assistance provided by the CZMA, as well as consistency requirements, have served as sufficient incentives to promote coastal management.

On the other hand, a number of other federal programs and policies influence coastal development patterns, and these are generally not coordinated and often work at cross-purposes. Federal subsidies for coastal development, for example, have arguably served to increase the extent of people and property at risk to coastal hazards and the degradation of sensitive coastal resources. Ideally, federal programs and policies should be modified to reduce development subsidies to discourage dangerous and destructive coastal development patterns, to coordinate and integrate federal programs and policies, and to enhance and support state and local coastal management efforts.

Federal coastal policy, we believe, can help to bring about more sustainable coastal development patterns. More specifically, future federal coastal zone management efforts aimed at sustainability should include the following action items:

- *Develop and implement a national coastal management plan.* Protection and management of the coastal zone is and should be a primary national goal. As such, the federal government should prepare a national coastal management plan, which could serve as the basis for, and the articulation of, national coastal management goals and objectives; could serve to coordinate the different programs, policies, and actions of many different agencies; and could identify a comprehensive management strategy and the necessary steps to ensure that our precious coastal resources and environment are preserved. The plan should take a longer-than-normal timeframe—at least 100 years, but perhaps 500 years.

Moreover, the national plan should address the coastal zone in a comprehensive fashion, considering federal actions and policies that occur on land but also near-shore and off-shore. For instance, the plan should seek to integrate the strategies and objectives of CZMA with those of sanctuaries.

- *Elimination or sharp reduction of subsidies for dangerous and destructive coastal development patterns.* Federal coastal management must include a critical assessment and modification of current development subsidies and programs that work at cross-purposes to sustainable coastal development. Among the specific program and policy changes which should be undertaken: Raising NFIP premiums to cover the true market value costs associated with coverage, incorporating a mandatory erosion control component as a condition of participation in NFIP, elimination of flood insurance availability in especially high-risk coastal locations (e.g., V zones within the 60-year erosion zone), elimination of casualty-loss deductions under the federal tax code, and raising the state–local cost share for disaster assistance (e.g., at least to 50% under FEMA's public assistance program). Coastal property owners should, we believe, be asked to assume, as close as possible, the full costs of locating where they choose. Moreover, coastal localities that choose to encourage or allow risky patterns of development, and make foolhardy public investments, should be asked to assume the lion's share of the costs associated with such decisions.

Enactment of the Coastal Barrier Resources Act (CoBRA), and subsequent expansion, represented an extremely positive change at the federal level but could be further expanded. Congress should consider "CoBRA-cizing" other sensitive coastal areas (e.g., development in or near wetlands, estuarine shorelines, sensitive habitat areas) and expanding the types of subsidies covered (e.g., bridges and other public investments which, though not in a designated unit, serve to induce development there).

- *Continue and expand funding and technical assistance for state coastal management programs.* The federal government has served an important role in facilitating and encouraging state (and local) coastal management through financial and technical assistance. These funds have been crucial, but also relatively meager. Efforts to expand funds will further enhance state management capabilities and will likely be repaid many-fold in terms of reduced property damages, reduced environmental destruction, enhanced public access, etc.

- *Expand focus on mitigation in existing programs; enforce existing protective programs more stringently.* There are a number of existing federal programs, policies, and regulations that have substantial potential for promoting long-term coastal sustainability. Major mitigation requirements exist, for instance, in the Disaster Assistance Act (e.g., Section 409 state mitigation plans) and could, if stringently implemented, do much to promote safer development patterns. A number of existing federal mitigation strategies, such as the 1362 flooded properties purchase program, could be expanded and used more effectively. The federal government, moreover, exercises direct regulatory control over certain coastal resources—for example, wetlands under Section 404 of the Clean Water Act. Such provisions could be enforced and applied more stringently (e.g., prohibiting all wetlands loss, prohibiting development in buffer zones, etc.). There are a number of mitigation and management provisions of existing federal laws that, consistent with the national coastal management plan, promote greater coastal sustainability.

- *Expand federal acquisition of sensitive coastal areas.* While the federal government is not in the best position to exercise direct regulatory control over coastal development, one of its most successful roles has been to preserve coastal lands through acquisition. The establishment of national seashores and wildlife refuges, for example, has resulted in the protection of large amounts of coastal land, setting important areas off-limits to future growth and development. Federal expenditures for acquisition (direct expenditures or grants to states) represent very efficient use of funds. Some expenditures, though initially costly, can serve to prevent significant federal costs later (e.g., through disaster assistance) and ensure that limited coastal resources are available to satisfy future environmental and recreational demands.

State Coastal Management

In the U.S. policy framework, states have taken the lead in the area of coastal management. We expect this pattern to continue, as states have both an appropriate geographical scale to consider many coastal issues and problems and the powers necessary to address them. Each coastal state will have a somewhat different set of management issues and programs, and somewhat different political and institutional structure, and the U.S. approach has allowed states considerable flexibility in developing their own appropriate management strategies.

State coastal management programs taken as a whole have accomplished much in the last two to three decades in encouraging more sensitive development patterns. There has been, however, considerable variation in state responses, with some states aggressively managing coastal growth and development and others adopting only the most minimal of management provisions. We believe that each coastal state must establish a minimum set of management requirements, within which local coastal governments might adopt more stringent or innovative requirements if they so choose. We believe states represent an important jurisdictional level for establishing and enforcing such standards and for undertaking certain management functions. Specifically, states can help to promote sustainable coastal development patterns in the following ways:

- *Establish minimum coastal development and planning standards.* Many states already do impose minimum development standards. We believe these standards should include prohibition of permanent shorehardening structures (e.g., seawalls, revetments, groins), erosion-based setbacks along oceanfronts, restrictions on building on or near dunes and dune fields, prohibition of development in coastal wetlands and wetland buffer zones, setbacks and other restrictions on development along estuarine shorelines, minimum stormwater management requirements, and minimum beach access requirements.

We believe that coastal states should implement these standards more consistently and more aggressively and should consider ways that existing standards may need to be tightened or expanded. For instance, even the impressive programs of states like North Carolina could be improved. While this state imposes a 60-year setback standard for large buildings, we believe a minimum 100-year setback is appropriate for all coastal states. Coastal states should also establish minimum local planning requirements, as many already do. Minimum state regulations are no replacement for detailed local comprehensive planning, and states should ensure that such local plans incorporate certain minimum components (e.g., planning for certain facilities and services, for certain hazardous areas, for hurricane evacuation and post-disaster reconstruction) and are faithfully implemented once adopted and approved.

- *Promote and facilitate strategic retreat.* States are perhaps in the best position to establish and implement a long-term shoreline retreat policy. In light of shoreline erosion and actual and predicted sea level rise, and the growing recreational and ecological importance of coastal areas, strategic retreat seems the most sensible and cost-effective strategy. Policies which armor the coastline and resist the forces of nature are largely futile and financially and ecologically costly. Where extensive development already exists (e.g., places like Myrtle Beach, S.C.; Virginia Beach, Va.; Ocean City, Md.) the "softer" approach of beach renourishment may be justified, although it is extremely costly and short-lived. These communities and their residents should be asked to assume the costs associated with not retreating.

  States can help to promote strategic retreat in numerous ways. These include many of the policies already mentioned, such as mandatory development setbacks, restrictions on shorehardening structures, and prohibitions on building immovable structures.

Some states, notably Michigan, have developed financial incentives to facilitate relocation of private structures. States should consider a range of programs to assist in relocation (e.g., a state relocation revolving fund, technical assistance).

- *Explore acquisition opportunities.* The aggressive coastal acquisition programs of a handful of states such as Florida and California suggest the extremely positive role such a strategy can play. Such programs can accomplish a number of objectives, including preservation of important coastal ecological functions, protection of important coastal biodiversity and critical habitat, reservation of lands for future public access and recreation, and prevention of exposure of additional people and property to coastal storms and flooding. States should consider establishing coastal landbanks, which could prioritize and acquire land well in advance and which could develop steady (and equitable) sources of long-term funding. (A number of sources should be considered, including land transfer taxes, hotel/motel taxes, sales tax, etc.)

- *Reduce state subsidies and development-inducing investments.* States should curtail subsidies and investments in the coastal zone, adopting their own state versions of CoBRA, and ensuring that public expenditures in the coastal zone (e.g., highway and road construction, beach renourishment) do not exacerbate hazardous and wasteful development patterns. Other states should take Florida's lead in adopting a set of infrastructure policies (under the 1985 Omnibus Growth Management Act) designed to reduce development pressures on barrier islands and high-risk coastal hazard areas.

- *Mapping and database assistance.* States are in an excellent position to develop the scientific databases and resource mapping essential for managing coastal development in a sustainable fashion. States are often in the best position to collect and analyze data on water quality, wildlife habitat, fisheries, and high-hazard risk zones, etc. Such efforts should focus on enhancing understanding of trends, on relationships between degradation and land use patterns, and on providing local governments and relevant state agencies with usable and accurate maps by which to make land use and management decisions. The federal government has also assisted in this regard and will continue to play an important role here as well (e.g., producing flood hazard maps under NFIP and funding research under the NEP, etc.), as will local governments. Especially important is the development of a statewide geographic information system (GIS), which could assist greatly in the simultaneous consideration of multiple resource values and in the integration of transportation, housing, land use, and other decisions affecting the coastal environment.

Local and Regional Coastal Management

Local government, perhaps more than any other jurisdictional level, has the potential to change conventional development patterns in coastal America and move human settlement patterns in the direction of sustainability. This is so for several reasons. Historically, land use decisions (e.g., zoning) have been viewed largely as a matter of local prerogative. It is at this level that officials have the management tools, and indeed the opportunity, to influence actual development projects and community-level land use patterns. While states can establish minimum development standards, consideration of detailed land use matters is neither technically nor politically feasible. So, much responsibility for detailed coastal management in the United States lies, and probably must lie, at the local governmental level. We believe that coastal localities have tremendous potential for reorienting coastal development and growth.

Specifically, we believe that coastal localities must embrace long-term sustainability as the overarching and unifying theme for all future planning and management. We believe there is much to recommend the vision of sustainable coastal communities, and in Chapter 8 we outlined and discussed in detail (which will not be repeated here) what we believe a sustainable coastal community is or could be. By way of summary, however, we do believe that sustainable coastal communities should seek to pursue the following:

- *Each coastal locality must have a sustainable community plan.* While many coastal localities have already developed land use or comprehensive plans, most have not adopted sustainability as a central goal, nor have they sought to manage or plan in a way which promotes sustainability. Very often such plans represent the most rudimentary classification of land uses and seem designed to facilitate or accommodate conventional destructive and wasteful growth patterns. Coastal sustainability plans would advance a different philosophy, one which seeks fundamentally to reduce the extent and amount of land development, to reduce the resulting human footprint, to reduce the extent of people and property at risk to hazards, and to minimize pollution and destruction of the natural environment.

Each local plan should include a sustainability audit as an initial step. Such an audit could include an analysis of the extent to which the community uses resources (water, energy, land), generates waste (water and air pollution and solid waste), places people and property at risk to natural disasters (e.g., amount of development in floodplains), and so on. Future land use and development decisions should then be judged and evaluated according to these important sustainability indices. Each plan should state the strategies and actions to be taken to enhance sustainability as gauged by these measures.

- *Moving beyond conventional zoning and land use controls.* Development in coastal regions is not unlike development occurring in many other areas of the country. It is characterized by low-density wasteful urban sprawl, highly consumptive use of open space and resource lands, and heavy dependence on the automobile. As well as being environmentally destructive, such patterns do not generally result in the creation of "communities" or built environments that are highly livable and which exude a sense of place. A major cause of these patterns is reliance on conventional zoning techniques which encourage the separation of different uses and the development of single-family detached units on large lots.

We believe that future coastal land use patterns should reflect a different vision, one which seeks to limit extensive low-density development; reduce the development footprint; funnel development and growth into, or around, existing towns and, where possible, promote infill and adaptive reuse; and promote mixed-use towns and cities that reduce use of the automobile, incorporate public spaces, and create a sense of place and community. Where possible, we believe, future coastal development should build on the existing network of coastal cities and towns before allowing development of outlying and undeveloped areas.

Coastal localities must critically assess their existing zoning ordinances and development codes to see how such patterns could be encouraged. Localities should explore a variety of potentially useful land use and development measures, including traditional neighborhood ordinances, urban growth boundaries, clustering standards, transfer of development rights, and land banks.

- *Integrative and holistic strategies.* The principle of sustainable coastal communities clearly implies strategies and approaches which are integrative and holistic and which look for ways of combining policies, programs, and design solutions to accomplish multiple objectives. Coastal localities can no longer look at transportation decisions in isolation of land use decisions, or affordable housing in isolation of environmental protection. Growth containment in coastal towns and cities can, for instance, reduce public facility costs, promote more affordable housing, and create vibrant communities. Such patterns can be furthered by integrating and coordinating decisions about transportation, land use controls, and a variety of other decisions. The idea of sustainable coastal communities also implies the need to view the community in terms of the resources consumed and waste streams generated by it. A sustainable coastal community is one which aggressively looks for ways to reduce water and energy consumption (resources generally in short supply), to reduce waste (air and water pollution, solid waste), to promote use of renewables (e.g., solar), and to promote recycling and reuse where possible.

- *Regional institutions and strategies will be increasingly important for sustainability.* As discussed in Chapter 7, many coastal resources and problems extend beyond local government boundaries and require regional solutions. Mechanisms for regional cooperation and planning in the coastal zone will, we believe, become increasingly important in the future. Use of mechanisms such as

SAMPs, estuarine management conferences (under NEP), and regional planning councils will become increasingly important, and local governments must increasingly be willing to assume or adopt a regional perspective where appropriate.

A Final Note: Defending a Collaborative Framework for Sustainable Coastal Development

In conclusion, it is clear that progress toward sustainable coastal development will require the concerted efforts of each jurisdictional level—federal, state, regional, and local. There is a natural tendency for some to call for a unified approach, one where coastal management responsibilities are invested primarily in one agency or jurisdiction. In the U.S. system of government this is infeasible politically and legally, and probably undesirable in concept. Each jurisdictional level has a special interest and contribution to make to coastal management, and much can be accomplished at each realm. Moreover, the coastal management collaboration must extend to the private sector as well, recognizing the important role played by such groups as The Nature Conservancy and the important influence and power exerted by banks and financial institutions, among others. While the collaborative framework is not without its limitations, it holds considerable promise, with the future directions proposed above, to move coastal areas toward sustainability.

Bibliography

Alexander, C. E., et al. 1986. *An Inventory of Coastal Wetlands of the U.S.* Washington, DC: NOAA.

Armingeon, Neil. 1991. "An Analysis of the National Estuarine Reserve Research System," in *Evaluation of the National Coastal Zone Management Program*. The Center for Urban and Regional Studies and the Department of City and Regional Planning, University of North Carolina at Chapel Hill, Chapel Hill, North Carolina.

Ballenger, Laurie. 1993. "In the Wake of Lucas vs. South Carolina Coastal Council: North Carolina's Oceanfront Setback Regulations." Ocean and Coastal Law Seminar, University of North Carolina at Chapel Hill Law School, Chapel Hill, North Carolina.

Barnes, R. S. K., ed. 1977. *The Coastline.* London: John Wiley.

Barth, Michael, et al. 1984. *The Economic Impacts of Sea Level Rise on the Charleston, South Carolina Area.* Washington, DC: U.S. Environmental Protection Agency.

Beatley, Timothy. 1991. "Use of Habitat Conservation Plans under the Federal Endangered Species Act," in *Wildlife Conservation in Metropolitan Environments* (Lowell W. Adams and Daniel L. Leedy, eds.). Columbia, MD: National Institute for Urban Wildlife.

Beatley, Timothy. 1992. *Hurricane Hugo and Shoreline Retreat: Evaluating the Effectiveness of the South Carolina Beachfront Management Act.* Final report to the National Science Foundation, September.

Beatley, Timothy, and David J. Brower. 1993. "Sustainability Meets Mainstreet: Principles to Live—and Plan—By." *Planning*, May.

Beatley, Timothy, David J. Brower, and Lou Ann Brower. 1988. *Managing Growth: Small Communities and Rural Areas.* Chapel Hill, NC: Center for Urban and Regional Studies, University of North Carolina.

Beller, W., P. d'Ayala, and P. Hein. 1990. *Sustainable Development and Environmental Management of Small Islands.* Park Ridge, NJ: Parthenon Publishing Group, Inc.

Berke, Philip. 1989. "Hurricane Vertical Shelter Policy: The Experience of Two States." *Coastal Management* 17, 193–218.

Black, Henry Campbell. 1983. *Black's Law Dictionary*, abridged, 5th ed. St. Paul, MN: West Publishing Company.

Booth, William. 1992. "Pre-Andrew Mistakes Are Being Repeated, Grant Jury Warns." *The Washington Post*, December 15.

Brower, David J., and Daniel S. Carol. 1984. *Coastal Zone Management as Land Planning.* Washington, DC: National Planning Association.

Brower, David J., et al. 1991. *Evaluation of the National Coastal Zone Management Program.* Newport, OR: National Coastal Resources Research and Development Institute.

Bunce, Leah, Jessica Cogan, Kim Davis, and Laura Taylor. 1993. "National Marine Sanctuaries: Critique in Light of the 1992 Amendments." April 15. (Unpublished classroom paper.)

Burby, Raymond J. 1990. "Reforming Relief: An Invited Comment." *Natural Hazards Observer* **XV** (1), September.

Caldwell, Lynton K., ed. 1985. *Perspectives on Ecosystem Management for the Great Lakes*. New York: State University of New York Press.

Carmichael, O.M. 1974. "Transferable Development Rights as a Basis for Land Use Control." *Florida State Law Review* **2**.

Carter, R.W.G. 1990. *Coastal Environments*. London: Academic Press.

Chabreck, Robert A. 1988. *Coastal Marshes: Ecology and Wildlife Management*. Minneapolis: University of Minnesota Press.

Christie, Donna, and Paul Johnson. 1990. "State Ocean Policy Initiatives in Florida." *Coastal Development* **18**, 283–296.

Clark, John R. 1977. *Coastal Ecosystem Management: A Technical Manual for the Conservation of Coastal Zone Resources*. New York: John Wiley and Sons.

Cogan, Jessica. 1992. "The Salt Pond Special Area Management Plan: An Experience in Bioregional Management." Department of City and Regional Planning, University of North Carolina at Chapel Hill, Chapel Hill, N.C. (Student paper, December.)

Conservation Foundation. 1987. *Protecting America's Wetlands*. Washington, DC: Conservation Foundation.

Conservation Foundation. 1990. *Protecting America's Wetlands: An Action Agenda*. Washington, DC: Conservation Foundation.

Costonis, John. 1973. "Development Rights Transfer: An Exploratory Essay." *Yale Law Journal* **83**.

Coughlin, Robert, and John Keene, eds. 1981. *The Protection of Farmland: A Reference Guidebook for State and Local Governments*. Washington DC: U.S. Governement Printing Office.

Coughlin, Robert E., and Thomas Plaut. 1978. "Less-Than-Fee Acquisition for the Preservation of Open Space: Does It Work?" *Journal of the American Institute of Planners*, October.

Culliton, Thomas J., et al. 1990. *Fifty Years of Population Growth along the Nation's Coast, 1960–2010*. Rockville, MD: NOAA.

Davies, J. L. 1973. *Geographical Variation in Coastal Development*. New York: Hafner Publishing Company.

Dean, Cornelea. 1992. "Beachfront Owners Face Possible Insurance Cuts." *The New York Times*, May 27.

Delaney, Richard F., David W. Owens, and James F. Ross. 1991. *Florida's Coastal Management Program: An Independent Assessment*. Prepared for the Governor's Office of Planning and Budget, July.

Dolan, Robert, and Harry Lins. 1987. "Beaches and Barrier Islands." *Scientific American* **257**, July.

Dressler, J. H. 1979. "Agricultural Land Preservation in California: Time for a New View." *Ecology Law Quarterly* **8**.

Duncan, Myrl E. 1984. "Toward a Theory of Broad-Based Planning for the Preservation of Agricultural Land." *Natural Resources Journal* 24.

Dworsky, Leonard B. 1988. "The Great Lakes: 1955–1985," in *Perspectives on Ecosystem Management for the Great Lakes* (Lynton K. Caldwell, ed.). New York: State University of New York Press.

Edgerton, Lynne T. 1991. *The Rising Tide: Global Warming and World Sea Levels.* Washington, DC: Island Press.

FEMA (Federal Emergency Management Agency). 1986. *Coastal Construction Manual.* February. Washington, DC: FEMA.

FEMA (Federal Emergency Management Agency). 1992. *National Flood Insurance Program Community Rating System Coordinators Manual.* July. Washington, DC: FEMA.

FEMA (Federal Emergency Management Agency). 1992a. "Statement of Operations." as of September 30. Washington, DC: FEMA.

FEMA (Federal Emergency Management Agency). 1992b. "Estimating Probabilities of Exceeding Given Levels of Flood Insurance Losses in a One Year Period." August 4. Washington, DC: FEMA.

FEMA (Federal Emergency Management Agency.) 1992c. "NFIP Financial Data and Related Information." Memorandum and information packet, September 2. Washington, DC: FEMA.

FEMA (Federal Emergency Management Agency). 1992d. "Coastal Communities with V-zones, cumulative total from 1978." Special computer run performed by FEMA for the author, November. Washington, DC: FEMA.

FEMA (Federal Emergency Management Agency). 1993. Data on the Community Rating System, provided by Cynthia Keegan, January 3. Washington, DC: FEMA.

Finnell, Gilbert L., Jr. 1985. "Intergovernmental Relationships in Coastal Land Management." *Natural Resources Journal* 25.

Flather, Curtis, and Thomas Hoekstra. 1989. *An Analysis of the Wildlife and Fish Situation in the U.S., 1989–2040.* Fort Collins, CO: U.S. Forest Service.

Florida Department of Natural Resources. Undated. *Inside the Florida Keys National Marine Sanctuary.* Tallahassee: Florida Department of Natural Resources.

Fox, G. M. and B. R. Davis. 1978. "Density Bonus Zoning to Provide Low and Moderate Cost Housing." *Hastings Con. Law Quarterly* 3.

Furuseth, Owen J., and John T. Pierce. 1982. *Agricultural Land in an Urban Society.* Washington, DC: American Association of Geographers.

GAO (General Accounting Office). 1990. "Flood Insurance: Information on the Mandatory Purchase Requirement." Report #RCED-90-141FS, August 22. Washington, DC.

GAO (General Accounting Office). 1992. "Coastal Barriers: Development Occurring Despite Prohibition against Federal Assistance." Report GAO/RCED-92-115, July. Washington, DC.

Godschalk, David R. 1979. *Constitutional Issues in Growth Management.* Chicago: APA Planners Press.

Godschalk, David R. 1984. *Impacts of the Coastal Barrier Resources Act: A Pilot Study.* Washington, DC: Office of Ocean and Coastal Resource Management, NOAA.

Godschalk, David R. 1987. "The 1982 Coastal Barrier Resources Act: A New Federal Policy Tact." in *Cities on the Beach* (Rutherford Platt, ed.). Chicago: University of Chicago Press.

Godschalk, David R. 1992. "Implementing Coastal Zone Management: 1972–1990." *Coastal Management* **20**.

Godschalk, David R., and Kathryn Cousins. 1985. "Coastal Management: Planning on the Edge." *Journal of the American Planning Association* **51**, 263–265.

Godschalk, David R., David J. Brower, and Timothy Beatley. 1989. *Catastrophic Coastal Storms: Hazard Mitigation and Development Management.* Durham, NC: Duke University Press.

Grenell, Peter. 1988. "The Once and Future Experience of the California Coastal Conservancy." *Coastal Management* **16**, 13–20.

Griggs, Gary B., James E. Pepper, and Martha E. Jordan. 1992. *California's Coastal Hazards: A Critical Assessment of Existing Land Use Policies and Practices.* Berkeley, CA: California Policy Seminar, University of California.

Gustafson, Gregory C. and L. T. Wallace. 1975. "Differential Assessment as Land Use Policy: The California Case." *Journal of the American Institute of Planners* **41**(6), 379–389.

Hagman, Donald, and Dean Misczynski. 1979. *Windfalls for Wipeouts.* Chicago: American Society of Planning Officials.

Hansom, J. D. 1988. *Coasts.* New York: Cambridge University Press.

Horton, Tom. 1991. *Turning the Tide: Saving the Chesapeake Bay.* Washington, DC: Island Press.

Houghton, J. T., G. J. Jenkins, and J. J. Ephraums, eds. 1990. *Climate Change: The IPCC Scientific Assessment.* Cambridge: Cambridge University Press.

Houlahan, John. 1989. "Comparison of State Coastal Setback to Manage Development in Coastal Hazard Areas." *Coastal Management* **17**.

Hout, Eldon. 1990. "Ocean Policy Development in the State of Oregon." *Coastal Management* **18**, 255–266.

Imperial, Mark T., Tim Hennessey, and Donald Robadue, Jr. 1993. "The Evolution of Adaptive Management for Estuarine Ecosystems: The National Estuary Program and Its Precursors." *Ocean and Coastal Management* **20**, 147–180.

Inman, D. L., and C. E. Nordstrom. 1971. "On the Tectonic and Morphologic Classification of Coasts." *Journal of Geology* **79**, 1–21.

Institute for Environmental Negotiation. 1991. *Management of Cumulative Impacts in Virginia: Identifying the Issues and Assessing the Opportunities.* Charlottesville, VA, December.

Intergovernmental Panel on Climate Change. 1990. *Climate Change: The IPCC Scientific Assessment.* New York: Cambridge University Press.

Joint Task Force on the Hazard Mitigation Grant Program. 1992. *The Hazard Mitigation Grant Program: An Evaluation Report.* Prepared by NEMA, ASFM, and FEMA. September.

Jones, E., and W. Stolzenberg. 1990. *Building in Coastal Barrier Resource Systems.* Washington, DC: National Wildlife Federation.

Kana, Timothy W. 1990. *Conserving South Carolina Beaches Through the 1990s: A Case for Beach Renourishment.* Charleston, SC: South Carolina Coastal Council.

Kaufman, Wallace, and Orrin Pilkey. 1979. *The Beaches Are Moving: The Drowning of America's Shoreline.* Garden City, NY: Doubleday.

Keene, John, et al. 1976. *Untaxing Open Space.* Washington, DC: Council on Environmental Quality.

King, Lauriston, and Steve Olsen. 1990. "Coastal State Capacity for Marine Resources Management." *Coastal Management* **16**, 305–318.

Klarin, Paul, and Marc Hershman. 1990. "Response of Coastal Zone Management Programs to Sea Level Rise in the United States." *Coastal Management* **18**, 143–165.

Knox, George A. 1986. *Estuarine Ecosystems: A System Approach*, Vol. I. Boca Raton, FL: CRC Press.

Kusler, Jon, et al. 1982. *Innovative Local Floodplain Management: A Summary of Local Experience.* Boulder, CO: Institute of Behavioral Science, University of Colorado.

Leatherman, Stephen P. 1989. "Impact of Accelerated Sea Level Rise on Beaches and Coastal Wetlands." in *Global Climate Change Linkages* (James C. White, ed.). New York: Elsevier Science Publishing.

Lippson, Alice Jane, and Robert L. Lippson. 1984. *Life in the Chesapeake Bay.* Baltimore, MD: Johns Hopkins University Press.

Lowry, Kem. 1990. "Ocean Management in Hawaii." *Coastal Management* **18**, 233–254.

Mandelker, Daniel R., and Roger A. Cunningham. 1985. *Planning and Control of Land Development: Cases and Materials*, 2nd ed. Charlottesville, VA: The Michie Company.

Manning, Billy R. 1988. "Building Codes and Enforcement by Coastal States and Territories of the United States." in National Committee on Property Insurance.

Merriam, Dwight. 1978. "Making TDR Work." *North Carolina Law Review* **56**.

Miller, H. Crane. 1989. *Turning the Tide on Wasted Tax Dollars: Potential Federal Savings from Additions to the Coastal Barrier Resources System.* Washington, DC: National Wildlife Foundation, April 17.

Millsap, B. A., et al. 1990. "Setting Priorities for the Conservation of Fish and Wildlife Species in Florida," *Wildlife Monographs*, No. 111, July.

National Commission on the Environment. 1993. *Choosing a Sustainable Future*. Washington, DC: Island Press.

National Committee on Property Insurance. 1988. *America's Vanishing Coastlines*, October. Boston.

National Research Council of the U.S. and the Royal Society of Canada. 1985. *The Great Lakes Water Quality Agreement: An Evolving Instrument for Ecosystem Management*. Washington, DC: National Academy Press.

Neal, William J. 1984. *Living with the South Carolina Shore*. Durham, NC: Duke University Press.

Nielson, C. A. 1979. "Preservation of Maryland Farmland: A Current Assessment." *University of Baltimore Law Review* 3.

NOAA (National Oceanic and Atmospheric Administration). 1990. *Biennial Report to Congress on Coastal Zone Management*. Washington, DC: Office of Ocean and Coastal Resource Mangement, April.

North Carolina Division of Coastal Management. 1988. *A Guide to Protecting Coastal Resources through the CAMA Permit Program*. Raleigh, NC: NCDCM.

NRC (National Research Council). 1990. *Managing Coastal Erosion*. Washington, DC: National Academy Press.

Nugent, Michael. 1976. "Water and Sewer Extension Policies as a Technique for Guiding Development." *Carolina Planning*, winter.

Palm, Risa. 1981. *Real Estate Agents and Special Studies Zones Disclosure: The Response of California Homebuyers to Earthquake Hazards Information*. Boulder, CO: Institute of Behavioral Science, University of Colorado.

Park, Richard A., Marrit S. Trehan, Paul W. Mausel, and Robert Howe. 1989. "The Effects of Sea Level Rise on U.S. Coastal Wetlands and Lowlands." Report No. 164, Holcomb Research Lab, Indianapolis, Indiana.

Perry, Dale, et al. 1992. "Hurricane Andrew—Preliminary Observations of WERC Post-Disaster Team." College Station, TX: Wind Engineering Research Council, September.

Petrick, John. 1984. *An Introduction to Coastal Geomorphology*. London: Edward Arnold.

Pilkey, Orrin, et al. 1980. *From Currituck to Calabash: Living with North Carolina's Barrier Islands*. Durham, NC: Duke University Press.

Pilkey, Orrin H., and Tonya Clayton. 1987. "Beach Replenishment: The National Solution?" *Coastal Zone '87*, New York: American Society of Civil Engineers.

Pilkey, Orrin H. 1989. "The Engineering of Sand." *Journal of Geological Education* 37, 308–311.

Pito, Vincent, Jr. 1992. "Accelerated Sea Level Rise and Maryland's Coast: Addressing the Coastal Hazards Issue." Paper presented to annual meeting of the Coastal Society, Washington, DC. April.

Platt, Rutherford. 1991. "Coastal Erosion: Retreat Is Often the Best Course." *Cosmos* 1 (1991), 38–43.

Platt, Rutherford, Timothy Beatley, and H. Crane Miller. 1992a. "The Folly at Folly Beach and Other Failings of U.S. Coastal Erosion Policy." *Environment*, November.

Platt, Rutherford, H. Crane Miller, Timothy Beatley, Jennifer Melville, and Brenda G. Mathenia. 1992b. *Coastal Erosion: Has Retreat Sounded?* Boulder, CO: Institute for Behavioral Science, University of Colorado.

Prichard, D. W. 1967. "What Is an Estuary, Physical Viewpoint?" in *Estuaries* (G. Lauff, ed.). Washington, DC: American Association for the Advancement of Science.

Prince, Harold H., and Frank M. D'Intri. 1985. *Coastal Wetlands*. Chelsea, MI: Lewis Publishers.

Reid, Walter, and Kenton Miller. 1989. *Keeping Options Alive: The Scientific Basis for Conserving Biodiversity*. Washington, DC: World Resources Institute.

Reid, Walter V., and Mark C. Trexler. 1991. *Drowning the National Heritage: Climate Change and U.S. Coastal Biodiversity*. Washington, DC: World Resources Institute.

Rogers, Spencer M., Peter R. Sparks, and Katharine M. Sparks. 1988. "A Study of the Effectiveness of Building Legislation in Improving the Wind Resistance of Residential Structures." in National Committee on Property Insurance.

Rose, Jerome G. 1975. "Transfer of Development Rights: A Preview of an Evolving Concept." *Real Estate Law Journal* 3.

Salmon, Jack. 1984. "Evacuation in Hurricanes: An Urgent Policy Problem for Coastal Managers." *Coastal Zone Management Journal* 12.

Salvesen, David. 1990. *Wetlands: Mitigating and Regulating Development Impacts*. Washington, DC: Urban Land Institute.

St. Amand, Lisa A. 1991. "Sea Level Rise and Coastal Wetlands: Opportunities for a Peaceful Migration." *Environmental Affairs* 19, 1–29.

Stickney, Wallace E. 1991. "Highlights of FEMA's Hazard Management Programs." Remarks made to Natural Hazards Workshop, July 15, 1991.

Stolz, James. 1990. "Preserving Open Land, Nantucket Style." *Country Journal*, November–December, pp. 24–27.

Stroud, Nancy. 1978. "Impact Taxes: The Opportunity in North Carolina." *Carolina Planning*, fall.

Thorne-Miller, Boyce, and John G. Catena. 1991. *The Living Ocean: Understanding and Protecting Marine Biodiversity*. Washington, DC: Island Press.

Thurow, Charles, William Toner, and Duncan Erley. 1975. *Performance Controls for Sensitive Lands*. Chicago: ASPO Planning Advisory Service, Report Nos. 307, 308.

Tiner, Ralph. 1984. *Wetlands of the United States: Current Status and Recent Trends*. Washington, DC: U.S. Fish and Wildlife Service.

Titus, James G. 1986. "Greenhouse Effect, Sea Level Rise, and Coastal Zone Management." *Coastal Zone Management Journal* 14, 147–171.

Titus, James G. 1990. "Greenhouse Effect, Sea Level Rise, and Barrier Islands: Case Study of Long Beach Island, New Jersey." *Coastal Management* **18**, 65–90.

Titus, James. 1991. "Greenhouse Effect and Coastal Wetland Policy: How Americans Could Abandon an Area the Size of Massachusetts." *Environmental Management*, November/December.

Titus, James, et al. 1991. "Greenhouse Effect and Sea Level Rise: The cost of Holding Back the Sea." *Coastal Management* **19**, 171–204.

Toner, William, et al. 1984. *Performance Controls for Sensitive Lands*. Chicago, IL: APA Planners Press.

Town of Nags Head, N.C. 1984. *Town of Nags Head, N.C. Land Use Plan 1984*.

Town of Nantucket, Massachusetts. 1990. *Goals and Objectives for Balanced Growth*, November.

Town of Surf City, N.C. 1984. *Town of Surf City, N.C. Land Use Plan* 1984.

University of North Carolina. 1984. *Review of State Programs and Policies to Reduce Coastal Storm Hazards*. Chapel Hill, NC: University of North Carolina Center for Urban and Regional Studies.

U.S. Department of Commerce. 1992. *Targeting National Coastal Priorities: Coastal Resource Enhancement Program*. National Oceanic and Atmospheric Administration, National Ocean Service, Office of Ocean and Coastal Resource Management, Coastal Programs Division, Technical Bulletin No. 105. July.

U.S. Environmental Protection Agency. 1991. *The Watershed Protection Approach: An Overview*. Washington, DC: EPA, Office of Water, December 1991.

Virginia Water Control Board. 1991. *Virginia Revolving Loan Fund: Program Design Manual*, revised. Richmond, VA.

Wells, John T., and Charles H. Peterson. Undated. *Ribbons of Sand: Atlantic and Gulf Coasts Barriers*. Washington, DC: U.S. Department of the Interior.

Zedler, Joy. 1991. "The Challenge of Protecting Endangered Species Habitat along the Southern California Coast." *Coastal Management* **19**, 35–54.

Index

About the Authors

Timothy Beatley is associate professor and chair of the Department of Urban and Environmental Planning at the University of Virginia. His teaching and research interests include environmental policy and planning, conservation of biodiversity, natural hazards mitigation, and environmental ethics. He is author of two recent books: *Habitat Conservation Planning: Endangered Species and Urban Growth* (University of Texas Press) and *Ethical Land Use: Principles of Policy and Planning* (Johns Hopkins University Press). He holds a Ph.D. in city and regional planning from the University of North Carolina at Chapel Hill.

David J. Brower is research professor in the Department of City and Regional Planning at the University of North Carolina at Chapel Hill. His teaching and research interests include coastal zone management, planning law, land use and environmental policy, growth management, mitigating the impacts of natural hazards, and sustainable development. He and Ms. Schwab are currently working on a planning law textbook. He has undergraduate and law degrees from the University of Michigan.

Anna K. Schwab graduated from the University of North Carolina at Chapel Hill with a law degree and a master's degree in city and regional planning in 1989. Since that time, she has worked full-time raising her two small sons and part-time as a research associate at the Center for Urban and Regional Studies at the University of North Carolina at Chapel Hill. Research projects with which she has been involved include coastal zone management, wetlands conservation, local land use planning, special area management planning, beach and shoreline access, sustainable development, the public trust doctrine, development on coastal barrier islands, wastewater treatment in coastal areas, wellhead protection, land banking, submerged lands, and planning and the law.